Printed in USA
Houston Public Library

"IT'S A SURE THING"

A Wry Look at Investing, Investors, and the World of Wall Street

Robert Metz

George Stasen

Illustrated by
Henry Martin

McGraw-Hill, Inc.

New York   San Francisco   Washington, D.C.   Auckland   Bogotá
Caracas   Lisbon   London   Madrid   Mexico City   Milan
Montreal   New Delhi   San Juan   Singapore
Sydney   Tokyo   Toronto

Library of Congress Cataloging-in-Publication Data

Metz, Robert.
    It's a sure thing : a wry look at investing, investors, and the
  world of Wall Street / Robert Metz, George Stasen ; illustrated by
  Henry Martin.
        p.   cm.
    ISBN 0-07-041778-4 (cloth)
    1. Stocks—United States.   2. Investments—United States.
  3. Stocks—United States—Caricatures and cartoons.   4. Investments—
  United States—Caricatures and cartoons.   I. Stasen, George.
  II. Martin, Henry, date.   III. Title.
  HG4661.M46   1993
  332.63'22—dc20   92-44803
                                                                              CIP

Copyright © 1993 by McGraw-Hill, Inc. All rights reserved.
Printed in the United States of America. Except as permitted
under the United States Copyright Act of 1976, no part of this
publication may be reproduced or distributed in any form or by
any means, or stored in a data base or retrieval system, without
the prior written permission of the publisher.

1 2 3 4 5 6 7 8 9 0   DOH/DOH   9 9 8 7 6 5 4 3

The sponsoring editor for this book was Caroline Carney, the editing
supervisor was David E. Fogarty, and the production supervisor was
Suzanne W. Babeuf. The book was set in Goudy by McGraw-Hill's
Professional Book Group composition unit.

Printed and bound by R. R. Donnelley & Sons Company.

This book is printed on acid-free paper.

The cartoon on the cover and in Chapter 48 is copyright © by
Henry Martin, originally in *The New Yorker*. Other cartoons by
Henry Martin, and copyright © 1988, 1989, 1990, 1991, 1992 by
Tribune Media Services, Inc., appear as chapter openers in Chapters
1, 2, 10, 36, 37, 39, 41, 42, 47, 51–53, 55–62, 64–69, and 71–75.

R0121993234
BUSCA

HOUSTON PUBLIC LIBRARY

To my beloved wife Liz, my eternal source of inspiration.
R.M.

To my daughters, Barbara and Wendy, for their patient trust in me. To my dear wife Patricia, for her enduring support and encouragement. Beyond measure, her indispensable contribution to my investment career was the sharing of her artistic vision that taught me how to break the mold and stretch my imagination.
G.J.S.

Contents

Preface

There are two kinds of surprises—the unexpected and the expected that fails to happen. It's the latter that best characterizes the U.S. stock market during the decade of the '80s. There should have been an exodus of individual investors from the market, but that didn't happen. Consider the negative forces at play.

As the '80s began, the stock market was still smarting under the legacy of the great '69 through '74 bear market, a classic by any standard. Then, in an effort to stifle rampant inflation, interest rates were driven to levels normally considered usurious. These rates were so high that they exceeded the historical returns from equities. With that relationship, who needed the risks and agony of the stock market? Individual investors should have embraced bonds in droves. Eventually, rates fell from their stratospheric levels, the national economy began to recover from a serious recession, and the stock market followed suit. However, another record waited to be broken on October 19, 1987, the greatest single-day decline in the popular stock market averages. If the confidence of individual investors needed a coup de grace, that was it. But there was no rush to the exit.

During the decade of the '80s, the number of individual shareowners actually increased by 70 percent. According to a New York Stock Exchange survey, 51.4 million individuals in the United States owned shares in a publicly traded company or a stock mutual fund as of mid-1990. Overall share ownership participation rose to 21.1 percent of all Americans. The stock exchange survey found that 34.1 million out of the 85.1 million households (with telephones) had at least one resident who was a shareowner.

What magnet could be so powerful as to overcome the record-breaking distortions of the '80s? There is no simple answer. It is well known that stocks have afforded the long-term investor an average compound annual return of about 12 percent. That in itself has a strong pull. However, in the decade of the '80s, the compound rate of return on the Standard & Poor's 500 Stock Composite Index was 17.4 percent. This return compares with compound returns of 12.2 percent for government and corporate bonds, 10.6 percent for commercial real estate, and 9.6 percent for money market funds. That's the magnetism of stock ownership.

Not only has individual shareownership increased despite serious challenges, the prospects favor further expansion. The two fastest-growing segments of the U.S. population are the post-WW II baby boomers and senior citizens. Present trends imply that both groups will substantially increase their participation in the stock market in the decade of the '90s. As women increase their position in the work force, their participation in the market should also increase. Finally, employee stock-purchase plans are becoming a powerful force in expanding public participation in equity ownership and in introducing individuals to first-time shareownership. It is to the relative newcomers that this book is dedicated. Library shelves groan under the weight of books devoted to the techniques of stock market investing. What is different about this book is its plea for plain common sense in equity investing and a belief that superior returns will follow its application.

The book has two parts. The first consists of 75 brief chapters, essays really, inspired by the accompanying cartoons by the noted *New Yorker* cartoonist Henry Martin. Each of these essays touches on some element of common stock investing. We hope you will find the usual investment jargon absent and the suggestions and advice user-friendly.

The second part, the stock evaluation checkoff list, may at first strike you as user-*un*friendly because it reveals the complexity of the equity decision-making process. However, that revelation should be more than offset by the organization of the decision process into its critical elements. You will quickly recognize what it is that you need to know to improve your odds for more successful investing.

We wish you good fortune.

Acknowledgments

While readers of *The New Yorker* have for many years enjoyed the gentle humor of Henry Martin's cartoons, they may not have recognized his special talent for finding humor in the world of finance. Hopefully, this book will correct any oversight. We consider ourselves singularly fortunate to have worked with this fine fellow.

Also, a word of praise for those associated with the nuts and bolts of the publishing process and their notable contributions to the birth of this book. First place belongs to Susan Gleason, our literary agent. Those who are fortunate enough to know and work with her realize that she raises the accolade "truly nice person" to new heights. Her dogged perseverance led to the good offices of its editor, Caroline Carney, whose enthusiastic support made it all come together.

Robert Metz
George Stasen

"Mr. McCormick is here to see you. He comes with a strong knowledge of financial markets and interest rate relationships and an offer to do lunch to demonstrate his interpersonal skills."

1

Trust Me!

Passing on the authority over your investment assets to a profes-sional, such as a broker, investment counselor, or financial planner, can be risky, but it also can make good sense—particularly if you lack a reasonable level of investment skills and experience. After all, there is nothing simple about investing and supervising your savings in the stock market. Another undertaking of equal complexity is hard to imagine. It isn't that the rudiments are difficult to grasp, but almost everything under the sun seems to affect investment performance in one way or another. What to do?

Consult experts, of course. After all, that's what one does when one's health fails or the Internal Revenue Service comes to call. There are more than enough investment professionals eager to serve your specific requirements. And, for the do-it-yourselfer, there is a wide variety of investment research and advisory services to call upon. But finding the right personal help is not all that easy. Here are some rules:

- *Rule 1: Be realistic.* Temper your expectations of what an investment professional can accomplish for you. Otherwise you may be told what you want to hear instead of what can be delivered within reason. Be especially wary of those who promise too much. You've probably heard how difficult it is for experienced money managers to beat the performance of the market averages. Believe it. The long-term records of the common stock mutual funds offer a sobering perspective on the range of performance possibilities.

- *Rule 2: Be prepared.* When you interview or check out enough professionals, it's going to strike you that they tend to sound alike in their sales pitches. That's no accident. After achieving a certain level of sophistication, these professionals go about their business in pretty much the same way with the same information. What's left to distinguish among them is their record of performance and the manner in which it is presented.

- *Rule 3: Be forewarned.* The experts would be less than human if they didn't attempt to put their best foot forward in soliciting your business. There is no scarcity of historical evidence to document investment performance, and there is always someone clever enough to put a seductive face on it. Wall Street continually produces "experts" who have recently outperformed or out-smarted the market. The trouble is the names are constantly changing. The few that do exhibit some longevity in the spotlight have their flat spots, too.

- *Rule 4: Be discriminating.* Where investment professionals really differ is in their attitude toward risk. Remember that it's your savings that are at stake. It's far easier for others to have a cavalier attitude toward the risk in your equity investments. Look for a good match with your own tolerance of risk.

- *Rule 5: Be honest.* Describe your investment objectives candidly. When retaining an advisor, some investors will describe themselves as completely conservative, but when speculative stocks are making their move, they are the first to complain about missing the action. Still others will claim they are seeking the excitement and high rewards in speculative stocks, only to be shocked when the risks materialize.

- *Rule 6: Be reasonable.* In an error-prone arena filled with uncertainty, losses are unavoidable. Resist the temptation to find fault. Tolerant clients will find their advisors trying harder. However, there is a limit to how many mistakes should be endured before the search for a new advisor is initiated.

Lesson
The experience of a professional does count for something. Good investing is an art of many compromises, and that makes the professional's prior experience especially valuable.

"In an effort to bring you more objective reporting, we will eliminate such words and phrases as 'took a nose dive,' 'plummeted,' and 'down the tubes' from our Wall Street roundup."

2

Damn the Averages

There is an almost irresistible urge to add drama to the reporting of stock market activity. Most times it is dull stuff. Keep in mind that stock market averages are merely mileposts. What investors really need is some vision of the market's future trend. That's the indispensable key to capital gains because few stocks will run counter to a broad uptrend or downtrend. But how often does the key work? Market forecasters predict and predict. Few, if any, succeed consistently. Talk about fiendish; it's mission impossible.

Consider the challenge. You start by looking at where the stock market has been, and from there you guess where it is going. The first step seems easy enough; it's history. But whose? Various indices will only occasionally describe the market's history in exactly the same way.

Over 5000 stocks are actively traded daily. Should you measure all of them, only the largest ones, or only a few industry leaders? Should you measure just the movement of their prices or their total market value based on price times shares outstanding? Or should you pretend that you've made equal investments in each of the stocks being monitored? And those are not all the alternatives. Market averages are based on diverse assumptions, and each assumption will paint a somewhat different picture of the market's current trend. With that uncertain beginning, it's time to face the future.

Most often, experts will project the market's future trend by extending the current trend. However, that brings to the surface another problem. Since the market never moves in a straight line, how much time best defines its current trend? Obviously, a day is too short, but is six months too long? Sometimes you can look back at the daily or weekly record of an average and see a clear trend. Sometimes not. What then? Some experts turn to statistical techniques, such as moving averages and least-square lines. O.K. Grant that the current trend may be a little murky, but where does the forecasting go wrong?

The factors that can affect the stock market's future path are almost beyond measure. They can be almost anything; they can range from international socioeconomic developments to company takeover bids. But, in a practical sense, they boil down to corporate earning power and what investors are willing to pay for it. It's tough enough for company executives to estimate earnings internally; it's even tougher for investors to guess from the outside. But the real backbreaker is what investors choose to pay for that earning power. Market history is replete with demonstrations of very wide mood swings between the reckless pursuit of gains and a mindless intolerance of risk—even in short time periods.

Essentially, the stockholder bets on the daily double of future earnings and how many times earnings the stock will sell for, that is, the price-earnings or P-E ratio. Success comes from being right on both judgments; failure, from being wrong on either. The stock market averages provide an imperfect gauge of how the race is going. But, without relating the price action on the trading track to earnings expectations, there is no way to tell if other investors are becoming more or less willing to accept risk. And that's precisely what you need to know. If the challenge seems formidable to you, you're on the right track.

Lesson
Remember, it's the big picture of the market's trend you're after, not the daily minutia. There is nothing magical about round numbers, resistance and support levels, advances and declines, highs and lows. The daily price swings provide mostly static when what you want is music. The popular market averages, such as the Dow Jones Industrials and the Standard & Poor's 500, have become such familiar fixtures on the financial scene that investors rarely think about their true usefulness. Actually, they put a blurred focus on short-term activity and reveal little about the future.

6

"With the stock market falling apart, suppose it becomes worthless? Then what?"

3

Good Question

Not just a good question, but a truly valuable question because it forces thinking about the unthinkable. It's all too human to emphasize opportunity and downplay risk in the stock market, but the risks, including extreme risk, are very real and need to be confronted occasionally.

For instance, the thought of a worthless stock market seems foolish, indeed laughable. Surely, unless the national political system were to collapse, there has to be some residual value in equity ownership. And surely there will always be those who are willing to step up and take a chance on it. That's right, of course. But, after a long decline in the stock market, it's hard to think about residual value and all too easy to be swept away by the prevailing doom and gloom.

Investors forget that serious declines set the stage for above-average profits. In a sharp and protracted decline, the common perception is that risk is rising, whereas risk is actually declining. Why else would history show that the stock market has turned around even while the accompanying economic news has continued to deteriorate?

The catch is in making your move too soon. That is where thinking about the unthinkable plays a role. Ask yourself, What is the stock market going to look like if it declines another 10 percent or so? What kind of news would make this a likely event? While zero value is beyond the unthinkable, what valuation would be acceptable to you under prevailing circumstances?

Unfortunately, there are no set formulas that unfailingly measure residual value. By hindsight, the pundits will point out that when the market bottomed it was selling at x times earnings, y times book value, etc. Market bottoms are not defined by these numbers. After the next serious decline, you will find a different set of relationships.

What makes the bottom of a severe market decline is simply exhaustion. The sellers give up. They see prices lower than the inherent value of their securities, even under drastic economic scenarios. At that point, the buyers will either join the sellers in their boredom or they will become aggressive bargain hunters. If the former, the experts will start talking about an L-shaped market recovery that drifts aimlessly for some time. Or, if the latter, the talk will be about a V-shaped recovery that moves sharply off the bottom. Remember, the sharper, the more traumatic and emotionally paralyzing the market decline, the greater the likelihood that the recovery will be quick and vigorous.

The biggest profits are found early in a market recovery so it helps to have a plan of action even if you decide to sit on the sidelines temporarily. Look for the signs of exhaustion. When news that ordinarily would put serious downward pressure on the market receives little or no reaction, it's time to think hard about the unthinkable.

Lesson
Superior investment returns are a function of disciplined thinking and well-controlled emotions. Near stock market bottoms, recognize that the current flows swiftly in the wrong direction. Most investors, unsettled by their losses and disappointments, simply will not confront the irrationality of their fears. That is what creates extraordinary opportunity for those able to take action.

"But before we get into specific buy-and-sell recommendations, I'd like to introduce our staff: Ed Simpson, our resident futurist; Myrna Franzek, our in-house seer; Ved Shandu, our staff prophet; and Madame Valesty, our senior astrologist."

4

Either...Or

Scoff if you will, but the futurists have the right idea. They are at least looking in the right direction and their approaches are different.

Stock market movements are based upon a continuous interaction of diametrically opposed opinions; that is, buyers and sellers are poles apart in their thinking. Small wonder then that the processes of making a decision are so varied. But there are mainstreams of analysis. The first is called the "fundamental approach." Adherents to this discipline emphasize the business as a business. The more details they can garner, the happier they are. Fundamental analytical techniques are fairly well standardized and accepted. The other common approach is called "technical analysis." Here, the emphasis is on the movements of prices or various other indicators of activity. The trick is to divine intelligence from the patterns of movements themselves and to compare these patterns to patterns seen in the past under what are assumed to be similar circumstances. Too often the beauty is in the eye of the beholder.

The probability is that the deeper you probe a company's fundamentals, the more confused or distracted you will become. Accounting nuances tend to hide or confuse as much as they reveal. Fortunately, those who make the buy-or-sell decisions, as distinguished from those who prepare the financial reports, are rarely bothered by such subtleties. Earnings as reported in the quarterly and annual reports are what count for them.

The basic argument supporting technical analysis is that everything that concerns a company, whether or not revealed, is reflected in its price action and trading activity. The flaw is that such analysis does not reveal which positive or negative forces are in the ascendancy. Consequently, the pattern to be traced out in time may be quite different from patterns seen in the past. "Forecast often" seems to be the motto of market technicians. Their iron-clad rule is "Never look back; don't complain and don't explain." What about the technician who consistently misses the mark? No problem. There's always another pundit ready for the limelight.

The challenge comes not so much in understanding a particular company as it does in making comparisons with the company's supposed peers. It's a mistake to think of any two companies as being alike, if for no other reason than they are managed by different people. You can group companies under a common heading, such as the chemical industry, but when you examine the individual companies it quickly becomes apparent that the differences between them are great—so much so that the "chemical industry" classification holds little meaning except for a common sensitivity to the business cycle. There seems to be virtue in extending the number of comparisons and relationships that can be made for any given company, but few of these hold up in the crucible of time.

The intent is not to belittle the work of the "fundamentalists" or the "technicians." Just don't take their words as gospel.

Lesson
Company and market data can help analysis a lot, but an accurate reading of the future is what counts. Since divining the future is no more than a best guess, investors must place heavy reliance on understanding current economic and business trends. The hazard is in placing too much reliance on the vision of the experts.

"Recession or depression? That is the question."

5

Charting the Unchartable

At first glance, financial charts seem to offer a road map to the future. Profitable destinations or dangerous pitfalls are easy to imagine. And, when the road turns into a detour, a charting enthusiast will shrug it off with a seemingly logical explanation and a new chart interpretation.

Chartists have their own jargon. For example, you will hear mumbo-jumbo about "resistance" levels and "support" levels. But, in practice, when these levels are pierced, they are supplanted with revised levels, without so much as a by-your-leave. Chart patterns are given meanings all their own. Trend lines emerge as if by magic. When subsequent realities fail to match up with projections, you can bet that a new pattern or new trend line will have emerged to explain the next projection. Chartists are ambivalent about the role of time. Some argue that it is irrelevant or distracting. For them, it's price and volume movements that count, and the emerging patterns, called "point and figure," are the key to future action. For other chartists, time is a critical ingredient because it's part of true history.

This is not to imply that charts don't have their place. They do. Charts permit masses of data to be summarized and presented in a suitable format. Sometimes valuable intelligence that otherwise would be missed becomes clearly evident. The trouble with charts is mainly in their interpretation.

For some inexplicable reason, the data, whether it is an economic statistic, a market average, or the price of a stock, is treated as if it has a life of its own. Keep in mind that regardless of what data is being displayed, it probably represents the summation of a wide variety of forces—some positive, some negative, and some currently neutral. Common sense tells you that with the passage of time, these individual forces will wax and wane. So it's possible for a chart to suggest relatively little change, when the underlying forces behind the data have changed radically. When the "why" of these changes is not analyzed, the data being charted takes on a life of its own. The popular stock market averages are a classic illustration of such deified data.

It sounds sophomoric to say that data trends continue until they change. What is meant by that is that the forces producing a trend must have been so powerful that the trend persisted until they were exhausted or other powerful, contrary forces intervened. Sometimes when a strong trend breaks, the reasons for the change are evident, sometimes they are not. Either way, strong breaks in trend deserve careful attention. The market is a rather efficient discounting mechanism, so it takes something highly unusual to knock it off course. Investors should be especially attentive when the market deviates sharply from its current broad trend. The wider the deviation, the more significant the signal.

Lesson

Charts serve well when they challenge our convictions and when they draw a useful historical perspective. They are particularly helpful when they highlight investor emotions by pointing to either overoptimism or overpessimism. However, the analysis of investment charts is an inexact art at best. Experience shows that forecasts based on charts are anything but precise.

"Just tell me the leading indicators are coming around and skip the dramatics."

6

Plain Truth

The overall performance of your stock portfolio will hinge mainly on the underlying trend of the market. Capital gains will prove illusive when investing against a downtrend, and large cash reserves will provide scant comfort when the market takes off on the upside.

Little wonder then that investors are constantly searching for signs and omens that reveal the market's trend. And, whatever investors want to know, suppliers of stock market data will give them all the minutia they can handle. Over time, countless bells, whistles, gauges, and thermometers of market activity have been concocted to satisfy the investor's true need and healthy curiosity. The question is, Do they help? The answer is an unqualified maybe.

At certain times, market indicators can tell you a lot. But, when are those times? They're when investor passions have become unbridled, and intellectual judgment has been overwhelmed by fear or greed. Never forget that the market is first and foremost a discounting mechanism. So there will always be occasions when bright or gloomy anticipations of the future incorrectly push investor emotions to excess. It is then that market indicators become very useful, particularly those that can be read as contrary to the current trend.

For example, when the market has been strong, you will find that surveys of investment advisory services record uniform bullishness on the market's outlook, and vice versa. When historically high levels of bullish or bearish sentiment are reached, it's time to plan for a change in market direction. Traditionally, the bulls look for higher prices, the bears for retreats—bull up and bear down.

Contrary indicators can serve two purposes. First, contrary indicators can help keep your own feelings in check. The last thing you want to do is follow the crowd when emotions are running high. Second, contrary indicators can force you to think against the grain—to look for outstanding bargains in market crashes and opportunities to sell at inflated prices when the market rockets.

What do you do about the indicators in the meantime? Knowing what the market in its many facets is doing day by day or movement by movement has its entertainment value, but rarely little else. Nevertheless, the assumption seems to be that if the indicators, such as the popular market averages, have occasional value, they should be constantly reported and explained. Remember that most of the time the indicators are recording unfiltered noise. Consequently, those running commentaries on why the market is rising or falling can be ignored at small risk, if any.

Where do you find serviceable indicators of the market's trend? Turn to your bookstore or library. Your time will be better spent in exploring the innumerable facets of stock market history than in being distracted by the market's daily meanderings.

Lesson
Whether you are reading the business news or checking out the market's indicators, confine your interest to the major developments. Search for evidence of changes that could counter current basic trends. Keep a lookout for developments so powerful that they suggest a turn may be close at hand.

"But, there's more to it than buying low and selling high."

7

Mastering
the Obvious

Timing is everything, the stock market experts will tell you. Don't tell me what, just tell me when, they are fond of saying. That might seem like oversimplification, but not by much. Actually, most investors concentrate on a dual goal, namely, selling at the top and buying at the bottom. This laudable objective goes by another name—the contrary opinion.

When most of the other investors are leaning strongly in one direction, contrary investors want to lean in the other direction. The flaw, of course, lies in thinking that the great majority of investors are always wrong, when, in fact, they are correct in major market moves upward or downward. Therefore, to be successful, contrary opinion investors must be highly selective when they employ their strategy.

Assume that you are looking at a hypothetical cycle. It starts down, bottoms, rises, peaks, and returns to the starting level. This could be a picture of the whole market or an individual stock. The first decision comes when approaching the bottom of the cycle. The sellers are becoming exhausted, and it's time for bargain hunting. There are two ways to proceed. Some investors prefer to let inherent value be their guide. Using the traditional measures, such as historically low valuations of revenues, earnings, and dividends, they look for the bargains that emotional selling provides. Other investors prefer to exercise patience and wait for evidence of a definite uptrend before making their commitments.

The second decision is called for when the rising trend is unmistakable and bullish attitudes are proliferating. If you are a truly contrary investor, you will take a profit and sell against the rising trend. By hindsight that could be a costly mistake. Your second decision should be to let the crowd join you as the movement from undervaluation to overvaluation progresses.

The third decision is mandated when serious overvaluation is reached. It's time to go against the majority by selling. Some investors set price objectives for themselves as a discipline. Others base their timing on the heat of the market. As long as it is pushing strongly upward, they sit tight; but at the first sign of real weakness, they liquidate.

Finally, as the downward trend takes hold, it is time to make the fourth decision and go with the flow. If you take a contrary stance here, you will be exposed to substantial losses as the downtrend continues.

Moving against the crowd sounds appealing enough. In practice, it's much more difficult. Market cycles contain much backing and filling, so the phases aren't clear. However, if you're disciplined, if you try to identify the cycles and act accordingly, you will be rewarded.

Lesson
Buying low and selling high sounds like the best-ever advice, but in practice there are four decisions to be made, not two. The objective is to know when to be in and out of step with the majority of investors. Selling and buying too soon can sabotage your performance.

"Two of the most fascinating scenarios have evolved from our economic analysis."

8

Pity for Pundits

Economic forecasters rationalize their positions as best they can. But, with so much ground to cover, so much sketchy data, so much that is unknowable, so much that must be qualified, so much that can't be articulated briefly, it's small wonder that they try to predict anything at all.

The advent of the computer was hailed as a boon to the art of economic forecasting. With it, massive amounts of pertinent data could be collected, stored, and processed with sophisticated statistical techniques. A new age seemed at hand. The activity was even given its own name—econometrics. Economists were courted and welcomed to the boardroom. The major investment research houses dangled their resident economists like Phi Beta Kappa keys. Hopes ran high. However, instead of retaining their lofty status, economists now find themselves in relatively low repute. What happened?

Whatever the true cause of their misfortune, it wasn't for want of trying. The computers were stuffed with statistics which their innards dutifully pounded and mashed, and out came the forecasts. But they were too often wrong, being barely better than blind tosses at a dart board. Economists almost seemed on sounder ground when they didn't have monster computer programs to rely on. In fairness, it must be observed that just about the time that the economists' tools were taking a giant leap forward, the business world began to undergo great change.

There's the lesson, as starkly as it can be drawn. Computers are absolute marvels at manipulating data so that decent insights can be drawn about the happenings of the past. But, for a forecast to be relevant, the future must look a lot like the past. When it doesn't, look out for trouble. That's what bagged the economic profession.

Still, some economists do have their moments in the spotlight. Just call for a major turn in the economy, and the media will come calling. Unfortunately, forecasters can be like stopped clocks—right for the wrong reason. Then, as time marches on, the honor of being right passes to a different clock.

Can economists give useful guidance? Certainly! They can tell much about the past and the current conditions of the economy. But the challenge they face is formidable. Take their forecasts with the proverbial grain of salt. Remember that the stock market itself has proven to be the best leading indicator of the trend of the economy. Its record as a prognosticator is far from perfect, but it's the best one available. That says a lot about the reliability potential of economic forecasts.

Lesson

Most often it's a safe bet that the economic future will resemble the immediate past. But when you bet your stocks on it, be prepared for some surprises. For the foreseeable future, economic forecasting remains an art rather than an exact science.

9

Something
for Everybody

Investors have every right to demand the impossible from their investment advisors. It's their money that's at risk. However, they have no reason to expect the impossible to be accomplished.

Demand the impossible? Well, if satisfying requirements at opposite ends of a financial spectrum meets the definition of impossible, that's exactly what investors should demand. To illustrate, consider the need to protect your investments from either the contraction of deflation or the erosion of inflation. These are clearly opposite objectives, though each is undeniably desirable.

Consequently, the first step in outlining an investment program is to define its objectives, even if they are mutually exclusive. You'll have to make judicious compromise. Admittedly, all tradeoffs are weak. You have to give up something in order to gain something. Investors must learn to live with that early on. While you might think that dealing with contrasting objectives would generate great frustration, it need not.

The greatest difficulty comes from trying to be honest with yourself about your investment objectives. If you want to protect your assets against the insidious inroads of inflation, stock ownership has been a traditional hedge. But you must be prepared to accept the price volatility characteristic of equities in that hedge. Your choice comes down to asset erosion protection versus asset integrity. Only you can decide which is most important.

Be open-minded about the alternatives. For instance, you are not limited to a choice between fixed income and equity securities. Investment hybrids, such as convertible bonds, which can be converted into common stock at a sell price, or preferred stocks, which are entitled to dividends even when the common stocks are not, may help you straddle opposing objectives. While you will lose capital gain potential, your offset should be less price volatility and superior income. There are many investment vehicles that will allow you to reach your goals through compromise.

In both bonds and stocks, you will find a variety of risk and opportunity. While quality is a concept somewhat hard to pin down, the differences between investments are tangible enough to afford you obvious choices. Opportunities are even more ephemeral, but they too will present categorical alternatives.

The danger is not so much in drawing the original plan as it is in changing goals in midstream. For example, in troubled times many investors will profess a strong desire for the capital preservation offered by fixed income obligations, but when the stock market turns hot, they discover that they're closet speculators at heart. Usually they'll switch goals at the wrong time and defeat their objectives.

Asking the impossible of your investment advisor is part of the game. Although perfection can't be achieved, a professional can come close if you clearly articulate your financial objectives and then stick to them.

Lesson
The drawing of a suitable investment plan is a matter of artful compromise. Well-thought-out diversification will bring the impossible close to reality. Consistency will bring its rewards.

"Arise, my love. Time to do options, sell short, merge, take over, arbitrage, wheel and deal, and all that kind of Wall Streety stuff."

10

Shades of Gray

Wall Street offers investors many and varied alternatives for the deployment of their savings. As the opportunities are diverse, so are the attendant risks. Whether recognized or not, everyone has a fairly well-defined tolerance of risk. Some experienced professionals suggest that you should never take investment risks that will disturb your night's sleep. Actually, it's a little more complicated than that.

Few investors are honest with themselves about their tolerance of risk. They will fearlessly barge into a red-hot stock market, and then with equal passion jump out at the bottom of a major decline. What they need is the realization that their tolerance for risk is poorly defined and at any given moment is mostly a reflection of the prevailing attitude of the crowd. However, what successful investment strategy demands is just the opposite—the loneliness of the investor who doesn't fear to stand alone. And that takes a discipline that does not come readily.

Risk tolerance should be driven not by the thrill of running with the crowd, but by changing personal circumstances such as age, position in society, or accumulated wealth. These should be the real limits on tolerance of risk. One would think that advancing age, rising position in society, and greater wealth would argue for greater emphasis on avoiding risk. And they probably do. However, the exceptions are worth thinking about.

Recklessness and speculation are thought to be the domain of the young. The argument goes that if all goes wrong, a person will have plenty of time to start over again. That's true in a sense, but it neglects the cold fact that savings available for investments are hard to come by in the first place. Eroded capital is hard to recoup. At the other end of the scale is the widow with her mite. "Safety first" would seem like the only appropriate motto, but that doesn't pay the rent or the grocer. High-yielding investments with marginal safety may be the only answer in her restricted situation.

Don't be lulled into a false sense of security when you make portfolio changes to lower risk. Recognize that you don't know and can't know all that you need to know to make truly sound decisions. The future may bring events that would have changed your strategy materially.

For those with sufficient accumulated wealth, the combined lure of freedom from taxes and the volatility of the stock market may seem too much to resist. But there is always the insidious erosion of savings' true value by persistent inflation. You needn't consult cost-of-living statistics, just watch the rising price of postage stamps for first-class mail.

Lesson

Tolerance of risk? "To each his—or her—own" applies, but only after honest soul-searching. No investment is without some risk. Sometimes the acceptance of higher risk is dictated by personal circumstances.

"Inexperienced investor? My new client thinks a liquid asset is money down the drain."

11

Small Purse No Curse

There is a first time for every investor, so don't let your lack of experience or the size of your savings deter you from making a beginning. Obviously, if it takes a broker the same time to service a large client as a small client, then large to small will be the pecking order for attention and service. Such is the way of the world. But remember that many large clients started when small and grew in stature. Make that your goal.

Most firms assign small accounts to junior members to give them experience. The objective is not so much to polish their investment skills as it is to teach them how to handle clients. Established firms are rightfully sensitive about their reputations and will carefully audit the activities of their junior members. You can turn your circumstance to advantage.

First, recognize that your advisor or broker will likely have more time to service your account. Second, your broker also will be anxious to enhance his or her personal reputation within the firm. Third, you should find your broker, with all that time to help, anxious to respond to your investment queries by digging through research files and tapping into the firm's resources in talent and support services.

The more successful investors will rarely be passive investors. It is imperative that you be self-reliant. Don't wait to be led by the nose. Use your eyes and ears to better advantage. The world is in constant change. Fresh opportunities for equity investors are being created all the time. Here are two true anecdotes that illustrate this point:

Many years ago, there was a rich wife who despaired of finding "something different" as her husband's Christmas present. A clerk in a fashionable store demonstrated a newly introduced instant camera. The gift was a real hit. The wife called her investment advisor and requested an opinion on the stock of the manufacturer, Polaroid. "Potential's attractive, but the stock's a rank speculation" was the reply. "Buy me some," she commanded. "If that camera can give my husband this much pleasure, it will be a big success." That holding grew to enormous size.

There was a pig farmer, a man of limited education. In the depth of the Great Depression, when the stock market was at its lowest repute, he did more than shop at his favorite store, Montgomery Ward. He talked to the clerks and the store manager. Would the company survive? he wanted to know. Assured of the answer, he sought a broker and began accumulating the shares of that retailing giant at under a dollar per share. The rest is history.

If you are a small investor, try to avoid following the crowd. Trust your powers of observation. Act as your own research department and from your daily experiences ferret out the opportunities. With the guidance of even a junior advisor or broker, you can make the difference between average and superior investment results.

Lesson

Being a small investor is not a handicap unless you make it so. Turn your position to an advantage, and don't let the penury of your purse stop you from thinking big. That's how fortunes have been made.

"Yes, Comstock, you founded Whiz Kid Computers, but your work habits don't measure up, so you're fired."

12

20/20 Foresight

Few would argue with the place in history belonging to founders of successful enterprises. For the most part, they were true visionaries. Despite an environment of intense competition, they either perceived an important need in the marketplace being ignored by others, or they conceived of products or services that would create demand. Either way, theirs were no small achievements.

Visionaries are difficult to identify. Some can articulate their dreams well and are spellbinders on the investment circuit. Others may be taciturn, but no less dedicated to the fulfillment of their aspirations. If you must make a choice, select a skilled communicator. In the company's early years, communications are all there is to support the stock in the marketplace.

If you are tempted to invest in an entrepreneurial endeavor, don't be blinded by the beauty of the vision or its potential for great rewards. Look instead for a management triangle. The visionary stands only at one corner of the triangle. At the other corners, look for the experienced businessperson and the financial expert.

True businesspeople have a wonderfully simplistic attitude. If the total cost of creating a product or service is less than the sale price, the difference is profit. In a young enterprise, it is the businessperson's role to keep the visionary's feet on the ground. Most visionaries hate detail, and they have innate difficulty appreciating the time required to move the company from point A to point B.

At the third corner of the triangle, look for the financial officer; finding a real Scrooge there would be a plus. Too often, the visionary and the businessperson are so engrossed with the corporate dream and the myriad of start-up details that the company's finances tend to be handled on a "fly now, pay later" basis. Repeatedly, raising capital is postponed with the excuse that when the company reaches some particular commercial or scientific goal, additional financing will be easier to find and will be less expensive. This naivete completely ignores the seasonality of corporate finance. When the winter winds chill investor interest to the numbing point, financing may not be possible, at least on favorable terms. The role of the financial officer is to make sure that the financial wherewithal is available to reach the company's objectives. Most likely, that means stepping on management toes. The history of ventures suggests that more enterprises fail because of inadequate financing than because of an improper dream or inadequate business acumen.

Once beyond the start-up phase, young companies face another hazard as they begin to mature. The casual mindset that typifies entrepreneurial activity must give way to the discipline characteristic of larger companies. Responsibilities must be diffused and departmentalized. The freedom to act individually is replaced with endless committee meetings. Some start-ups make the maturity transformation without difficulty, but some otherwise promising companies fail. Watch for signs of a slowdown from expected progress. Also, remember that the challenges of this transition period frequently entice the company's founders to sell the company to a much larger one at a substantial premium over current market prices.

Lesson
Business visionaries capture the limelight with the excitement of their ideas. But, as a potential investor in a vision, look for evidence of a qualified management team that can turn vision into reality.

"So then I told my investment counselor that any damned fool could combine limitless opportunity with unquestioned safety."

13

Safety Risk

The investor is like a hunter shooting at moving targets from a bobbing boat. Worse than that, the targets are on both sides of the boat. Constant change is both boon and bane to the investor, and trying to hit opposing targets is enough to give anybody fits.

Diversification is the means of calming the investment waters and discriminating among many targets. Diversification is not only *a* solution, but *the* solution. Just one problem though. How much diversification is enough? The answer lies somewhere between betting the ranch and owning countless financial bits and pieces.

A good beginning point is the gulf between investment safety and outright speculation. You can choose one or the other, but with diversification you can have some of both. The enormous variety of investment alternatives provides countless ways of satisfying your personal tastes and requirements. It's like having your cake and eating it too. But you just knew that there had to be a catch somewhere, didn't you? You're right!

Investment markets are more homogenous than you might at first realize. Every day the media report the winners and losers in the stock market. It's like being at the track, and race after race being out of the real money. But it's not a market of winners and losers; it's a market where mass psychology is the name of the game.

If you were to examine the price action of the vast majority of stocks over a long-enough time period and ask what factor most influenced their performance, the answer would lie in the basic trend of the market. In other words, stocks go with the flow; there are few exceptions. What moves the basic trend of the market? It will be either earnings or what investors are willing to pay for those earnings. Most often, the answer is the latter. Therefore even a highly diversified portfolio fails to offer much immunity.

The prices of fixed income investments also act pretty much as a group by moving opposite to the general trend of interest rates.

If rates fall, bond prices move up and vice versa. As a general rule, bond and stock prices move in opposite directions, on the basic assumption that cheaper borrowing costs stimulate business and costlier borrowing constricts business.

It should be clear that while diversification is beguiling, it is difficult to achieve. While there are other alternatives—international investments, precious metals, and collectibles, for example—beware of similarities in the basic trends. Breaking an investment portfolio into tiny bits and pieces in the search for safety may not seem counterproductive, but it can be that.

Lesson
True diversification is hard to achieve. The major portfolio building blocks tend to move in the same direction at the same time. That severely limits the protection that diversification affords. Recognize that the building and deployment of cash-equivalent reserves is probably your best diversification tool.

"Edith, we've been wiped out in the options market, so I've opted for Buenos Aires."

14

Grasping for Gain

In high school physics class, you learned about that wonder of wonders, the lever. Employ a little effort with a lever, such as a crowbar, and you get a larger return for the same amount of applied energy. Practical applications of the leverage principles abound and seem universally virtuous. But when applied to the financial arena, leverage has its failings.

Investment leverage takes many forms, some of which may be practical, such as a mortgage on your residence, but others, such as options on stocks, stock indices, and commodities, may be outright dangerous. In the real world, if you try to lever out a heavy rock with a prybar and fail, the rock sinks back to where it was. Not so with investment leverage because it works both ways. When you borrow funds to increase the capital gain potential of your portfolio—it's called buying on "margin"—you are exposing yourself to a serious potential for capital loss. When financial leverage fails, the rock sinks lower and becomes harder to retrieve. The road to great wealth lies in using other people's money, say some of the newly rich. There is some truth in what they say. What they don't say is that the same road in the other direction can lead to poverty.

Sophisticated equity investors approach their responsibilities with considerable humility. They've learned that they can't know everything that will affect the value of their investments. More importantly, they recognize that they cannot know what they need most to know—namely, what lies in the future. Consequently, mindful of these limitations, they consider financial leverage as only somewhat enhancing an opportunity, and as substantially increasing a risk.

If you add the increasing volatility of the market caused by program trading, it becomes hard to justify maintaining a margin account. With appalling speed, computer models detect small differences within the market or between markets. Equally fast, computers generate buy and sell orders and maneuver massive amounts of capital. The problem is that most of the activity takes place at the same time and in the same direction, thus increasing volatility as well as your risk of a margin call.

However, margin leverage is tame compared with the leverage of options, be they commodity, monetary, financial, or individual security. For investors insensitive to risk, options markets represent the happy hunting ground of unrestrained speculation. Big risks are offset by big rewards, or so it seems. But, as with most games of chance, the game is biased to favor the house.

Option markets are in reality two markets, wholesale and retail. This arrangement stems from an honest effort to smooth out some of the wildness inherent in options leverage. Thus traders on the floor can trade not only on behalf of the retail customer's account, but for their own accounts. On the face of it, that seems reasonable until you realize that the trader's cost of doing business is much smaller than the customer's cost. Therefore, the options floor trader not only stands at the center of activity but can respond more quickly and at lower cost to changes in market tone.

Financial leverage in any form is enough to make the inexperienced investor financially ill at some time or other. Plan to rise high on your learning curve before you are even tempted.

Lesson
Don't let hope for large rewards blind you to the risks. Enlarging your portfolio through borrowing or other forms of leverage is a two-way street. Be ever mindful of the added risk from today's volatile markets.

"If you want my opinion, the stock market could go up or go down, unless it just goes flat."

15

It's a Fact

Strong differences of opinion make the market. When a trade takes place, a buyer and a seller have agreed on the present value of some security. However, on the sidelines, you will find diverse opinions that surround that transaction. They belong to the "almost" sellers and "almost" buyers who lack the will to act at the security's present price. Should you explore their views, you will find yourself coming round full circle. Conflicting opinions are easy to come by on Wall Street.

Given the massive amount of information that can affect investment decisions and the profit to be drawn from experience, it's wise to turn to the experts for advice. The catch is that if you turn to enough of them, you will soon be receiving conflicting advice. One will recommend buying what the other recommends selling. It happens all the time. So what do you do then? Obviously, more opinions don't help, they only compound the confusion. To make it even worse, these conflicting judgments are pretty much based upon the same set of facts.

Consequently, seeking too many opinions is a vain exercise. Instead, when you are asked to consider a recommendation, probe deeper into the "why" of it. When you find experts who can rationalize their opinions in ways that build your confidence in them, you are well on your way to a fruitful relationship. Real experts know why they believe what they believe; more importantly, they can articulate their positions in language you can understand.

It helps you to be reasonable in your expectations of the results that experts can deliver. Investment advice can never be certain. When you hear of a "sure thing," be wary. When promises of performance are well above average, run, don't walk, to the nearest exit. And don't be overly impressed with a fancy office and a prestigious reputation. What you should seek is the right personal "chemistry."

Too many investors play musical chairs with their experts, be they brokers or investment counselors. If the experts fail to meet certain performance expectations during some short time period, the investor severs the relationship. Think about it. If trained investment professionals can take the same information and come up with diametrically opposed conclusions, doesn't it follow that expert advice is bound to fail from time to time? Investment relationships are too infrequently given the patience they require to develop.

Remember that relationships with advisors should be mutually satisfactory. The tyrant client gets poorer results, not better. The overwhelming majority of investment advisors are anxious to please, and they take satisfaction in their professional performance. You can help your own cause by being patient, reasonable, and consistent about your investment objectives.

Lesson

In the investment arena, conflicting expert opinions are the name of the game. Safety in numbers is an illusion. Until you can build confidence in your advisor, search hard for the "why" of his or her recommendations.

"Mr. Smithers, don't think of it as a loss of capital, think of it as a whopping opportunity to lower your taxable income."

16

Enduring
Another's Toothache

Wall Street has raised weasel wording to an art form. Never say "will" when you can say "may." Always choose "seems" or "appears" over "is." Say "eased" instead of "dropped." Use "modest" in place of "substantial." Choose "aggressive profit taking" over "sharp decline." Never a "retreat," just a "pullback." Etc., etc., etc.

You have to sympathize with the professionals. They serve in a business where it is easy to be wrong—often. It's not their fault; it's the nature of the business. But nobody likes to be wrong that often. So bring on the language hedges. The trouble is that the practice is so ingrained in the investment profession that it becomes a refuge for sloppy thinking.

Investors have no choice but to demand plain speaking from their advisors. Unfortunately, on the other side of the coin, some financial experts see ambiguity as self-defeating. You'll find their opinions firm, unwavering, sure, and convincing. They become adept at selling their point of view. Or is "overselling" a better description?

The truth is that most investors can benefit from the motivation and push that a salesperson can supply. Where investments are concerned, there is too much room for procrastination. There is a saying about putting in a golf game that goes "Never up, never in." The same is true of the money game. Timidity is costly.

But there is more to it than evasive language. Take a recommendation to buy—or one to hold, or one to sell. That's straightforward enough. However, in practice you will find a need for additional shading. Between a "sell" and a "hold," there is room for a "strong hold." A stock may have gotten ahead of itself in price, but it still represents good value overall. Between a "hold" and a "sell," there's a niche for the "optional hold." Maybe the reasons aren't potent enough to justify selling a stock, but, relative to other opportunities, it should be regarded as a logical source of funds. Remember that investment decisions are an amalgam of positive and negative elements, and it's tough to put a label on the final judgment.

There's another reason why recommendations are rarely hard and fast, and that's the role played by the time horizon. For instance, a recommendation to sell a stock might be based on the momentary anticipation of an unexpectedly disappointing earnings report. But the same stock, using a slightly longer time frame, might be rated a "strong hold" in recognition of its valuable assets.

The temptation to hedge opinions about investment matters is irresistible, but it is frequently overdone. Admittedly, value judgments and timing decisions are laced with uncertainty. Nevertheless, if you have misgivings, press on until you reach the level of plain speaking.

Lesson

Euphemisms are an inseparable part of Wall Street's jargon. Be forewarned, and take the hedging with good grace. Most times, it is not the product of calculated deception, but rather the way information is communicated in an uncertain environment.

*"I am happy to announce that this year the annual report will be devoid
of words like 'dipping,' 'falling,' 'plummeting,' 'plunging,'
and 'crashing.'"*

17

No Thanks
for the Memories

Here's a tip that is almost guaranteed to put you one up on the
experts. It's all too human for investors to remember smashing successes and painful losses. Over time, these memories coalesce into

a mass of prejudices and biases that cloud what would be otherwise straightforward decisions. Memory becomes confused with reason. Only long experience with this fault would reveal how common and costly it is among even disciplined professionals.

Perhaps some illustrations would help drive the point home.

Suppose that the earnings record of Company X has been erratic, to put a good face on it. Then the company undergoes a complete management change and its outlook becomes much more predictable. Reasoning tells you to take a closer look, but memory says, "Forget it; it's been a loser."

Suppose that a company which has traditionally offered "me-too" products at discount prices decides to acquire or invent a first-line product offering to be sold at a premium price. Memory says that the company's efforts in the past don't hold out much hope for success, but reason says, "Take a look; this is different."

Suppose that a well-run company has a poorly managed competitor who's notorious for undercutting established prices. Eventually the discounter fails and pricing firms. Memory says, "No thanks, poor industry margins." Reason says, "Look again; it's a new deal."

Suppose that a company that has traditionally offered a "me-too" product line initiates a radically different, innovative advertising campaign around a radically redesigned product line. Memory says, "Their promotions didn't work in the past, so why bother?" However, reason says, "Look at what would happen to the bottom line if the company were able to increase its share of market."

Suppose that a company has been so successful that it has managed to dominate its domestic market to the degree that its growth rate slows. Then it begins to repeat that performance in international markets. Memory says, "Mature company," but reason says, "It's a fresh start."

Suppose that a company is introducing a breakthrough technology but finds this takes much more educational effort than was planned. Memory says, "Management failed to meet its own set goals." Reason says, "Marketing is delayed, but not derailed."

These illustrations are overly simplistic, but the advice is not. Don't let memory control reason. Watch for opportunities to apply this adage, and you will find yourself on a route to above-average investment returns.

Lesson
When you take a look at an investment recommendation, always give it a fresh, unprejudiced look.

"Vintage year! We can tolerate some extravagance for the annual meeting. Hire the Philadelphia Orchestra."

18

Stop the Music

Managements of publicly traded companies are burdened by an accountability that private company managements can ignore with pleasure. While both must shepherd shareowners' resources, public company managements are required to present their efforts in an honest light to the investment community. That sounds easy enough, but it isn't. Furthermore, when management ineptly discharges this responsibility, it's the shareowner who foots the bill.

Investor-relations styles cover the gamut. Some managements are tight-lipped and report only what's absolutely necessary. Some managements lose no opportunity to ballyhoo everything, including a regular dividend payment. Some choose deliberately to deceive. Somewhere in that range is a golden mean, impossible to find.

Why impossible? Because some company news developments are open to either negative or positive interpretation. Say the company's quarterly report is disappointing. A detailed revelation of the causes might indicate the end of an unusual problem, but on the other hand, such a revelation might be interpreted as a weak excuse and a cover-up. How does management tell its story without being misleading? The answer is sometimes with skill and sometimes with great difficulty.

Obviously, investor-relations programs that are too weak or too strong are not only wrong, but, fortunately, easy enough to spot. It's the middle ground that presents the difficulty. "Stocks don't go up, they are put up" is an old Wall Street axiom—meaning that without some promotion stocks tend to languish, certainly relative to other stocks that are being properly promoted. Consequently, it's prudent to find out who's in charge.

For the largest companies, you can assume that their investor relations are sophisticated and well organized. For the smaller companies, it's different. Sometimes the company contact will be a Streetwise individual who will be helpful and informative. That's reassuring. Other times, a call to investor relations gets transferred around. If that happens, give up; you already have your answer. Sometimes newer firms choose to delegate the responsibility to professional investor-relations counselors to offset their inexperience in handling the financial community. That's smart. In any event, do some digging, because the quality of investor relations affects how well the company's stock will perform.

Where does the danger come in? Obviously, it's in overpromotion. Once a promotional campaign gets going, it is hard to stop. Since company executives usually hold stock and/or options in their firms, they are not disinterested spectators. One of the common danger signs is overexposure. Watch for too much of a company's material in your mail. Be alert when the company is mentioned far too often in the media. Another danger sign occurs when a promotion-minded company suddenly becomes quiet. Most likely, bad news is in the wings. And another symptom of danger is delayed news. When business news is positive, it's out fast. When poor, it's invariably late.

Even legitimate promotion can have its dangers. There's the risk that too many fair-weather stockholders will be attracted to the company—stockholders who will sell in a rush at the first sign of disappointment.

Lesson
Make it a point to learn how a company handles its investor relations. If the answer isn't obvious, do research. Look for a positive company attitude, but be sensitive to dangers of over-promotion.

"Herbert! Wouldn't our money be working harder if you just eliminated the dogs and weak sisters from our portfolio?"

19

Working Money

"Is my money working?" is a proper question for any investor to ask. The answer will depend upon how "work" is defined. In simplest terms, you have only two alternatives when putting your money to "work." You can choose either to rent your savings or to become the part owner of a business. If you do the former, you can anticipate that interest is being earned daily at a fixed rate and in this sense money is "working." If you do the latter, a well-protected dividend paid quarterly serves the same purpose.

But that's only a partial answer to the "working" question. For the same period of time, publicly traded investments are fluctuating in their value to other investors. Consequently, it's the combination of the interest or dividend rate plus the change in current price versus cost price that determines how hard the money is really "working." That is what is meant by the term "total return."

When you rent your savings via some fixed income obligation, you want assurance that not only will interest payments be made on time but funds will be available to return your principal on maturity. Quality ratings on bonds offer good guidance that this "work" will meet your expectations. However, there is little correlation between quality and potential price changes, since the economic forces that determine interest rates will override quality considerations. Bonds are every bit as capable of providing a negative total return as stocks.

When savings are risked in business ownership, the confusion deepens. Ask the question for equity investments—Is my money working?—and the answer will probably depend on how well the stock's price has performed. Instead, attention should be directed to the company's performance as a business. For instance, is the company meeting its stated goals and how much of that is being translated into net earnings? In actuality, investment returns are anchored more to the swings of investor opinion than to business fundamentals. Nevertheless, business as business is the "work" that rates your concern.

The failure to keep the priorities right creates opportunity. When a stock fails to perform as well as the market, it becomes a "dog" in a portfolio. If it is a laggard in its price action too long, it becomes a candidate for outright sale. There is little patience for the stock that represents a good business performer and a poor market performer. The sad fact is that too many stock portfolios are treated as a source of entertainment. How hard the company is working at its business doesn't seem to matter. That impatience generates many a fine investment opportunity.

Cash equivalent reserves are often maligned as not "working." The fact is that when the bond and stock markets are both in declining trends, reserves are the hardest-working investments in the portfolio because they are not deteriorating in value and when ultimately reemployed should buy cheaper and larger positions.

Lesson
Total return measures how hard your money is working, but price changes are only part of the explanation. Consider what's happening to the business. Your money may be working harder than you realize.

"Now then, all those in favor of our picking ourselves up, dusting our-selves off, and starting all over again, say 'Aye.'"

20

Wrong Again

The only thing worse than making a serious investment mistake is refusing to admit it. Presumably, the faster mistakes are corrected, the less they cost. That's the theory, at least. However, all errors in judgment are not alike. In the stock market what may appear as an error may not be an error at all. To illustrate. Suppose that after careful research you buy a stock, only to have the market hit one of its infamous sinkholes. Now you have a painful loss, and you're wondering all too naturally if you too should join the crowd by running for cover and building reserves. Clearly, market psychology has soured, but pause long enough to ask yourself if the company's fundamentals are still intact. If so, take heart. It should become apparent that your malaise is the product of your hindsight, not your foresight. Too often, investors embrace the adage, "Cut your losses and let your profits run," without thinking through the soundness of that advice. There is nothing in the world to prevent a loser from becoming a winner and vice versa. If the company's fundamentals are sound and expected to improve with the passage of time, ease off.

Far too many investors regard all their losses as mistakes. However, if you decide that you have indeed made a serious error in judgment, do more than recognize it, correct it. Unfortunately, inexperienced investors will too often take their cash from a liquidated position to the sidelines rather than take advantage of the bargains made available in a demoralized market. Usually, they will hang on to their "mistake" and eventually sell out at a market bottom when hope seems to have been abandoned. Some use their experience as an excuse to quit the market while others retreat only to be enticed back into the market at substantially higher levels. Consistent participation in the market is a prerequisite for successful investing.

Most experts will advise the stock market investor to keep some reserves for just such an eventuality. The trouble is that just when those reserves should be growing to their maximum size, there will be an even greater temptation to commit them to a hot stock market. On the flip side, you can be sure that when those reserves have achieved their greatest usefulness in a market downdraft, the appeal of holding cash-equivalent reserves will be stronger than ever.

If you find yourself constantly liquidating carefully researched commitments, recognize that you are not confessing to errors in judgment but to a lack of patience. Put as much care into the rationalization for a sell as you gave the original buy. Chances are that you will be surprised by the opportunity that lies in remaining in the position you were about to liquidate.

Lesson

The careful management of cash reserves is one more illustration that mental discipline is the key to achieving well-above-average returns. When you recognize a mistake, correct it.

"Mr. Jamison's portfolio has suffered another downward adjustment."

<u>21</u>

Take It or Leave It

You don't have to be a long-time stock investor before you find yourself getting emotionally involved. Try as you will to be dispassionate about your portfolio performance, you will most likely fail.

Your stocks will take on a personality of their own. Profitable holdings become favorite pets, while the losers are relegated to "dog" status. Everybody does it. You are not alone. It's so interesting to weigh portfolio "winners" against the "losers." Unfortunately, this natural inclination introduces a serious flaw, most often overlooked in the management of positions. In theory, successful investing should be a well-disciplined intellectual activity, but in practice it isn't.

A truly expert investor once suggested that investors should become well versed in trading postage stamps before being allowed to trade common stocks. The point made is that because it's hard to become emotionally attached to colored scraps of paper, one concentrates instead on the forces that increase or decrease their value in the marketplace. Not so with common stocks. The "winners" are quickly cloaked in all sorts of rationalizations that justify the retention of these holdings; an emotional bond is formed. And, the better the performance, the stronger the bond. When the appropriate time for a position's sale has been reached, that bond must be broken.

True opportunity in a stock occurs when the current price is substantially cheaper than the real value per share. When the converse is true, it's time to sell. Think of it only as bartering away some item that has lost its appeal or usefulness for you. Some investors experience difficulty in selling stocks at a loss. Emotions are at work here. It's not easy to concede defeat. But, realistically, things do go wrong; the unexpected does happen. The question should be "Can the capital that remains be made to work harder elsewhere?" In other situations, the emotions make disappointment slave to impatience. Few business timetables are actually met. Force yourself to distinguish between transient developments and change in fundamentals. You can safely assume that other investors share your impatience. The real test is whether you can turn their impatience to your advantage.

Many investors seem to develop their strongest emotional entanglements with stocks that hold promise of great rewards. Being in on the ground floor of a potentially huge development sets a bond that is almost impossible to break. Swallowing "pie in the sky" is a common failing.

Lesson
Giving a stock a personality is a common, if human, error. Trouble follows when there is a divergence between image and reality.

"Couldn't I have a hint instead of the usual nasty surprises?"

22

It's News

Developments in the stock market provide more than a few jolts to unsuspecting investors. Even the weakest foreboding of what is to come is better than a costly surprise. Unfortunately, the hints are few and far between. Fear of the unexpected is what keeps investors glued to the financial news, even when it is irrelevant.

For a better perspective on the worth of current events, stock market participants should read a stack of year-old financial newspapers. They will be struck immediately by how much of the day's sound and fury was later dissipated. Even worse, they will note how much sound and fury proved entirely misdirected. Excursions and alarms make the news, but who bothers to report that the resulting anxieties were fruitless? Read long enough and you will come to the conclusion that most of what passes for daily financial news has little immediate value. But it *is* entertaining.

Admittedly, some daily developments take on a special significance. Money supply, trade balance, currency exchange data, earnings reports, etc., can influence the short-term trend of the market when first announced. However, the announcements with the greatest impact are those that were least anticipated. Very quickly, these announcements are factored into stock prices, so there is precious little time to react. Fretting over them later contributes nothing.

Especially frustrating are those fragments of information that leave you thirsting for more. For example, a federal tax increase appears imminent. But how much of an increase? In which areas? What do you do? The answer is probably nothing. News of this kind shifts around almost daily. Besides, developments like these are so long in unfolding that they may be already discounted in stock prices. Contain your concern.

On occasion, you will find developments that can be crucial to a personal investment decision. There's the challenge. How often and how intently should you follow the financial news for that once-in-a-while event? The radio receiver is an excellent model for you to emulate. Its antenna can collect a wide variety of signals, but in its innards are circuits designed to strip away the static and turn noise into intelligible sound. Your chore is to discriminate between entertainment and significant information amidst the deluge of financial news.

The first step is to curb your appetite for investment information. More is not better. It's worse. You will never be able to handle everything available. The trick is in determining what is important to you and your own process for making decisions.

Financially important news gives the appearance of driving stock prices. Soon mild interest in developments deepens into a love-hate relationship with the news. That's dangerous. Investing in the stock market is an intellectual exercise. Short-term profits and losses are most often determined by events that cannot be foreseen. Why become overwrought with news developments? That merely clouds your vision of what happens next, which is where real profit lies.

Lesson
It's all right to be entertained by the financial news. Admit it, but discipline your appetite for it. Distinguish between truly significant investment developments that affect you and the entertainment that the media so liberally provides.

"I see investors shifting their preferences for high-priced and low-priced stocks."

23

Big-Picture Painters

Wall Street has a penchant for sweeping statements. Growth stocks are in! Small-company stocks are out! Service stocks are in! Finance stocks are out! And on and on. In the never-ending search for ways to simplify equity selection, generalizations have become the tools of the trade.

Unfortunately, the generalizations too frequently fail to serve the purpose intended. The primary reason is that the labels don't fit very tight. If the generalizations have validity, the stocks of an industry or conceptual group should move up and down together. The fact is, they don't make good traveling companions.

The utility stocks are a good example. For decades, they were held in investors' portfolios for their relative price stability and generous dividend yields. As a group, they were mainly sensitive to changes in interest rates. When interest rates rose, utility stocks fell and vice versa. But even then there were important differences in utility stocks. One of the biggest was geography. Some areas of the nation were economically stagnant, while others were enjoying a boom. That meant that some utilities had much less need for retained earnings and could pay out high dividends, whereas others had to conserve cash to meet heavy plant and equipment expenditures. Individual earnings growth rates became a valuation factor.

Some of the differences were more subtle. For instance, utilities were, and are, a regulated industry. In some areas, rate-setting commissions were notoriously penurious or slow to act, while others recognized the need for high service rates in order to support future expansion. The source, price, and reliability of a utility's fuel made for still other differences. And when the nuclear generation emerged, other distinctions were established. At first, nuclear power generation was thought to be a boon, but then costs went out of control and it became a bane. Note also how environmental concerns affected utility company operations differently.

Finally, when you look hard enough, you will find that most industry or conceptual groups, such as the utilities, further break down into separate subgroups. Some utility companies sell only electricity, some natural gas, some water. Many provide varying combinations of electricity, natural gas, water, and like services to their customers, so when utilities are lumped together, much is overlooked.

There's no denying that there are cycles among groups. Especially by hindsight, they seem to fall in and out of favor. Swings in the popularity of the gold group illustrate that well. But, as a practical matter, by the time it becomes clear that some group is "hot" or "cold," much of the profit has been made. The probabilities are that whatever may have been the merit in the original idea, its value will be overblown eventually. Curiously, these sweeping generalizations take a long time to burn out.

Lesson

Despite a lack of homogeneity, industry and conceptual groups are part of the market's lore. Trading between sectors will continue to have its adherents. Ignore the siren song and concentrate your attention on finding an advantage.

"So my stock tip was wrong. Forget it and take your vacation."

24

Give It a Rest

Investment portfolios suffer from more than the ups and downs of the market. They also suffer either from their owners' excessive concerns or from outright neglect. Usually it's one or the other because balanced oversight is difficult to achieve.

If a stock portfolio is well structured, it should not require intense supervision to achieve good long-term results. Assuming that you have developed a set of reasonable expectations for the holdings, only those developments that materially alter these expectations should merit your attention. Such developments should prove infrequent. As for neglect, the other extreme, ignorance is not bliss. Expectations have a way of not materializing, or not materializing as and when expected. However, even if your investment portfolio were managed at some golden mean of attention, something most likely will be missing—an emotional distancing, a vacation of sorts.

As individual investments age, they are sorted into "winners" and "losers." That trait is so universal that it's an intrinsic part of Wall Street thinking. It's so human to fall in love with the winners and to despise the losers. Consequently, portfolio management, which begins as an intellectual exercise, turns into an emotional one. It becomes increasingly difficult to sell a winner and all too easy to dispatch a loser. What's needed is a regular vacation from investment emotions so that your attention can be refocused.

Start by impassively examining the business expectations for each company in your portfolio. Market gyrations and the price swings of individual stocks make it easy to lose sight of the underlying fundamentals. More importantly, price frenzies make it even easier to forget that all investment returns lie in the future. The past is history. In the stock market, it is never clear whether the past is a prologue or a point of departure. There's plenty of agony in a winner-turned-loser, and real exhilaration in a loser-turned-winner. Clean your emotional slate. Picture how your individual investments are positioned relative to your own anticipation of what lies ahead.

Don't be distracted by minutia, for it's the big perspective you're after. Reexamine the forces driving each business toward success and the obstacles that could lead to disappointments. Ask what needs to happen to influence other investors. After all, it is they who will ultimately determine your profit or loss. How confident are you of your appraisal? Are more research and questioning appropriate? Only when you are satisfied that you have sufficiently established the background data, should you address your price goals.

Portfolio vacation time is the ideal opportunity to set new price limits. Question whether you would buy your "winners" at today's prices. Would you buy your "losers" at their current price if you didn't already own them? Force yourself to choose prices at which to sell, add, scale back, or even short a position. It's easier said than done, but you will find the discipline worth the effort.

Experience will teach you how frequently your portfolio needs a vacation. The correct timing will depend upon how the market has been acting. When it has had a strong move, it's time to check the emotions. The market's own vacation time, a period of relative stagnation, will prove the best time of all, because then it's easier to think than act.

Lesson
Give your portfolio a break. Occasionally, throw away your "winners" and "losers" preconceptions. Forget the past and concentrate on the future.

"Chief says you've done wonders with the financials, but they still don't zing."

25

Cooking Books

Investment decisions are tough enough without having to worry about accounting alchemy. Fortunately, public companies must comply with government regulations that require the timely filing of detailed quarterly and annual financial statements. These safeguards work well, despite a few glaring lapses from time to time.

Financial statements are mostly history, particularly by the time they are printed and distributed to shareowners. However, they can provide the clues to future developments, and that's what makes them worth some study. Moreover, you don't have to be an expert in accounting niceties to derive value from them. Hear what management has to say, but make it a habit to check out the fine print. The law requires full disclosure, but information that's embarrassing to company management does not have to be set in bold type. It can be disclosed in an inconspicuous place under the assumption that there it probably won't be read.

The law permits considerable latitude in a company's disclosures to the public, so you will find statements that range from exhaustive to minimal, from promotional to cryptic. Keep in mind that it's clues to future earnings that you seek. While managements rarely make their earnings projections public, some are not beyond coloring the company's horizon a rosy hue. When business progress is not meeting expectations, watch carefully for rubber numbers. The temptation is especially strong for the managements of "hot-stock" companies. It's tough moving out of Wall Street's limelight. Too often, reported earnings and earnings potentials are stretched to fit the hot-stock image. That's not exactly fraud, but when the hard realities finally emerge, it's disaster time for the shareowners.

At the other extreme are company managements so paranoid about embarrassment before the financial community that they meet only the minimum requirements of public disclosure. They usually take conservative accounting to an extreme. Nothing illegal here, but the shareowner is affected nonetheless. Investors have demonstrated their indifference over and over to the quality of earnings, at least in the short run. Consequently, understated earnings and minimal disclosure combine to lower the company's market value at the shareowner's expense.

Between the extremes is the company management that makes clear and full disclosures. In the annual reports, such a management makes five-year comparisons of vital statistics. These help investors spot deviations in important trends. Often management will go a step further and explain anything unusual. These techniques and others that make annual reports easier to use are positive signs of a management's forthrightness and sensitivity to a shareowner's needs. Look for that kind of management.

The nature of some businesses makes for erratic earnings comparisons. To counter this, some managements make accounting adjustments to control quarterly fluctuations in the hope all can be brought right in their fourth quarter. While the disclosures are less than perfect, their intent is noble enough. But sometimes this tactic leads to painful adjustments at fiscal year-end.

Managements are in a position to see the disappointments coming. Some respond by lowering analyst and investor expectations in advance of their normal reporting date. Better that than a sharp price reduction later, which would bring with it challenges to management's credibility. But other managements will tough it out, hoping for some offsetting news to develop. It's a deadly sign when companies delay their financial reporting. Inevitably, it's bad news that causes the delay.

There is more to financial reporting than outright number trickery. Management attitudes toward public disclosure vary widely. Search for companies sensitive to their shareowners' need to know.

Lesson
The peril lies not so much in hidden financial wizardry as in failing to search thoroughly enough for clues to the company's

future. Be critical in your reading of company annual reports. Managements are required to make "full disclosure" to their shareowners, but there is considerable latitude in how the revelation is delivered.

"If Trend Dee, Inc., will propose a two-for-one split, knock three times."

26

Miraculous Piece of Pie

Stock splits are miraculous in the sense that they produce something out of nothing. But while a split gives the shareowner more shares, that only means that the same size piece of shareowner pie has been cut into smaller pieces, and the stock's price immediately falls to reflect the split. Bottom line, there should be no difference between the presplit or postsplit value of the shareowner's holding. Actually, there is more to it than that.

Stocks are split for several reasons. For example, the stock's price may have climbed to a lofty level. Many investors have an aversion to high-priced stocks, so the lower price of the split shares accommodates their preferences.

Often, company managements rationalize that the additional shares will make it easier to attract new shareowners while retaining the old. By building a much broader shareowner base, the company paves the way for a future equity financing. More shares outstanding also promote higher trading volume. In turn, higher trading volume implies some dampening of the stock's volatility. Less volatility is a plus because it appeals to most investors, especially those who invest for the long term.

Additional shares may make it easier for larger investors to establish their initial positions. As trading activity picks up, some of the presplit shareowners may be induced to take profits and scale back their holdings. That creates supply for interested institutional investors.

Another common reason for a split is that a company's management may be anticipating a surge in earnings. By diluting the surge over a larger number of shares, management draws less attention to the bulge in earnings. Thus a stock split in some instances can be a harbinger of better things to come. All these reasons increase the attractiveness of a stock, which should ultimately be reflected in higher prices.

However, stock splits have their flip side. Stock splits become more numerous as a strong market advances. The popularity of splits induces some companies whose shares are priced low to follow suit, as a boon to their shareowners. However, when the uptrend reverses, the split price of these stocks may fall below critical levels at $10 and $5 per share. At $10 or below, many institutional investors lose interest and sell their positions. At $5 or below, the shares fall into the "penny stock" category and are further shunned. While such treatment may be unfair, that's the way it is.

The announcement of a stock split sometimes precedes the announcement of equity financing. When you hear the news, it's time to question if the company would benefit from a fresh infusion of equity capital. Most stocks will suffer if the new financing will mean dilution, no matter how worthy the purpose.

Generally speaking, stock splits are a healthy sign and are undertaken by companies at a moment of strength. To split a stock at a time of weakness is to ask for trouble because it takes time to move the new shares into the hands of long-term holders.

Lesson
Technically, stock splits may not appear to give you something for nothing. But stock splits are more than nothing. Frequently, they have positive implications that manifest themselves over time.

"Stock prices slumped today. The Dow Jones Industrial average fell 29.31 points. Prices of precious metals plunged. Yields fell on CDs. I tell you, it's a laugh a minute around here, Ed."

27

Seller's Market

It's worth remembering that your fellow investors have widely differing motives when they decide to sell a stock. Many of these motives have little or no bearing on a stock's intrinsic worth. For instance, some investors may want to take a loss simply to offset a previously established capital gain so as to reduce their tax burden. Others will sell because they are bored with a stock's performance relative to the market. Still others may need to cash in for noninvestment reasons—for example, to raise funds for a business. And so on. It is wise to think of these various motives when you are tempted to follow the herd by selling out. If the stock is in a downtrend, don't jump to the conclusion that other investors know more than you do and that the company's fundamentals have lost their attraction. Remind yourself that for every recorded transaction, the seller is matched by a buyer.

The way that the antics of the stock market are reported you might be led to think that the market participants are of one mind. Reassure yourself that they cannot be if transactions are to be consummated. Nevertheless, market breaks have a scary quality about them, like a truck rolling downhill without brakes.

One explanation for the often-made observation that market declines are much rougher than market climbs lies in the probability that on the downside investors sell for many reasons that are not related to an individual company's long-term prospects. Keep in mind that there are market mechanics that play an important role in exacerbating a decline that are absent when the market makes its opposite reaction, a steep rise. For example, there are margin calls, that is, requests from brokers to those owning stock bought with borrowed money to either add fresh capital to their account or to sell holdings to bring down the level of borrowing. This forced liquidation accounts for many of the big price drops characteristically seen at the bottom of a steep decline. They should be seen as an invitation to bargain-hunt and not as an inducement to join the fearful herd.

If you can resist the mental pressure, severe market declines offer an opportunity to pick up real bargains. But don't be too early. Sharp discounts from previously higher prices can be a snare because they are so enticing. Remember, this isn't a question of something with fixed value being reduced to bargain prices. Prices discounted from unrealistic levels are no bargain at all. In a substantial market decline, the selling usually comes in waves. Selling climaxes come only after the sellers have become exhausted. If you find yourself getting bored with bargain hunting as the market continues to decline, the odds are that the market is near a true bottom.

Lesson
When the stock market crashes, and the fear of further decline is widespread, think not of the risk but of the opportunity to bargain-hunt. Further slippage in the market averages may come. Steel your resolve. The careful judgments that you make can prove rewarding.

"Just tell the stockholders that our anticipated profit surge will start from a lower level."

28

Elusive Goals

Some business managements exercise a hidden talent that deserves fuller exposure. That's the talent for making excuses to fit the shortfalls in attaining their previously stated goals.

Whatever the problem, they always seem to have an explanation handy.

Unforeseen troubles do occur, and sometimes they occur in bunches. Managements' crystal balls are not any clearer than anyone else's. So there are times when the excuses offered can be taken at their face value. For example, unforeseen swings in currency exchange rates occasionally cause embarrassment for multinational companies whose business activities were otherwise on projected targets. But it's when the excuses don't ring true or when they become habitual that you should be on your guard. There are telltale signs.

Shortfalls and disappointments frequently come purposely wrapped with an emphasis on "good" news, like new products, aggressive marketing campaigns, or overhead-reduction programs. The general theme is "Today may be bad, but tomorrow will be so much better." Occasionally that's true, but you're on safer ground if you assume the worst and search for a better alternative.

Another dead giveaway is the paper blizzard tactic. When you find your mail overloaded with company releases that add up to little more than "Shareowner, we love you" messages, be forewarned. Sheer volume is meant to compensate for content.

Bad news is at times accompanied by the announcement of a management shake-up. That's the "they did it and they're gone" ploy. That may be true, but did the company's management also explain what took so long for them to wake up? Be suspicious, the incompetents may still be in charge.

When you encounter a string of excuses, beware of the chronic underachiever. For these companies, things not only go wrong, they seem to go wrong all the time. The excuses proffered will border on the imaginative and lack candor. Avoid commitments to these companies at all cost. Few stocks will perform well if a company's management lacks credibility with investors. Remember that once credibility has been destroyed, it takes a long time to be reestablished. Meanwhile, the stock will find little support during market downdrafts.

It's all too human to hate being wrong. Consequently, some managements paint their corporate goals in the lightest pastels. Almost everything they say is carefully hedged. That way they avoid altogether the embarrassment of making excuses. Too much hedging is a poor sign. Investors can't expect perfection in business performance, but they are entitled to clearly defined goals.

What distinguishes an above-average management is the ability to call the shots and then deliver. That means they have kept their goals within their grasp. Failures are infrequent and excuses seldom presented. As you familiarize yourself with the company, you will likely find not only excellent management but attractive economic fundamentals. Look for these companies; they make for solid long-term investments.

Lesson
When corporate goals elude management, exercise your impatience. Some forbearance with disappointments may be justified, but put yourself on the alert when offered excuses for underachievement.

"Reflecting our more aggressive policy, clients' accounts gained last month, on average...not counting, of course, those that expired under the strain."

29

Portfolio Athletics

High portfolio turnover has its advocates. For them, the short term is everything. It isn't that they don't regard themselves as serious investors. It is simply that they regard time as the enemy. Wait too long, they reason, and you're inviting something to go wrong. They watch their portfolios intently and when price objectives are reached or when something unexpected happens, they're smoke, they're sold out. On the flip side, their profit objectives are usually quite modest and, in that sense, their expectations are realistic.

What's wrong with this approach to managing a stock portfolio? First off, nothing. For some portfolios managers, this technique seems best suited to their personalities. Unfortunately, when their portfolio returns are ranked against their turnover, it's hard to find an advantage to the frenzied activity. In fact, the relationship may be an inverse one, which is to say the higher the turnover, the poorer the performance. There are several explanations.

Investment markets are fraught with impatience. It's natural for the participants to seek quick, if not instant, profits. And when these profits can be compounded, that's real frosting on the cake. But in a general sense, these expectations are unrealistic. You know that when too much attention is focused on the same immediate goal, the opportunity is diffused. Think of time as an ally, not as an enemy.

Where high-turnover investors go wrong is that they assume that because many other investors are passive they can take advantage through prompt action. There are several difficulties with the "quick on the draw" point of view.

For instance, when news is released about a company, can you be sure how the stock will react? If, as often happens, the news can be interpreted as either good or bad, where's the advantage in acting fast? There are occasions when bad news is later tempered by a convincing explanation of the particulars.

At other times, developments may have been anticipated and adequately discounted in the price of the stock. In fact, stocks have been known to rise on bad news, such as a dividend cut, and fall on good news (see Chapter 41). Sometimes the news isn't news, it's just a rumor. What if the rumor turns out to be false?

Sometimes bad news is subsequently overshadowed by good news. What do you do then? Will you have the courage to reverse your sell decision and buy back your previous position? Most investors prefer to bury their chagrin and search for another alternative.

If you choose to join the frenzied crowd, be prepared to pay close attention. Constant scrutiny seems meritorious, but have you asked yourself how you will distinguish between valuable and valueless information? Most of the information passed around Wall Street is more properly classified as noise. It takes extraordinary skill to distinguish between the two in the near term.

Lesson
Don't make the mistake of confusing portfolio activity with progress toward investment goals. Being a successful short-term investor is much more difficult than it appears.

"Memo to the Chief Economist: No more trend lines!"

30

Another View

We all love labor-saving devices, and, for the investor, it is hard to beat a chart on that score. So much useful information can be assembled in a small space. But, no matter how tightly packed the data, there's always room for deception, and that's the rub. Some of the deception is self-induced, but sometimes charts are designed to deceive.

Charts are their most effective when used to present a single element, such as the day's hourly temperatures. There is no arguing with the information conveyed. Suppose that hourly humidity readings are added to the temperature readings to make up a temperature-humidity index. Now you can see the record of the "discomfort level" as it rose and fell. But what made the index move the way it did? Was it the temperature, the humidity, or both? The chart can't tell you. Financial charts record a much greater complex of elements in their displays.

Economists and market technicians plaster whole walls with charts of this and that. Charts are the tools of the trade. The trouble is that after a while the chart takes on a life of its own. The underlying forces driving its movements are ignored or forgotten, and that's plainly dangerous.

What you want from a chart is insight to its true meaning and some reasonable indication of where its readings may be headed. But if the underlying forces are shifting in strength, how can you develop conviction about the next direction? Most often you are left with a sometimes serviceable picture of history and very weak clues to the future.

Investors should be wary of reading more into a chart than is there. Sometimes, when the patterns seem so familiar and clear, the charts can be the most deceptive because changes in the underlying forces are not appreciated. It's hard to believe that a strong uptrend or downtrend will be interrupted, but that happens regularly. Therefore, while charts can capsulize volumes of data, their usefulness is limited in understanding the essential forces at work.

Charts can also be used to purposely deceive. For example, by using only part of a range, the readings can be made to appear much more dramatic than they would be otherwise. Long periods of time can be collapsed into a small space, creating an illusion that time was hardly a factor. Starting a chart at a deep trough in the readings can also create the impression of substantial upward movement. The tricks are many, so be on your guard.

A chart can be particularly informative when its readings are compared against some standard yardstick. For instance, if the performance of a particular stock is pictured against the performance of one of the popular market indices, you not only see whether it was superior or inferior, but you get a feel for its sensitivity to market trends. On the other hand, without a standard of comparison, a stock's performance might appear attractive, yet be deceptive.

Lesson
Charts are essential investment tools, but never forget that they have their limitations. Common mistakes are to read too much intelligence into their patterns and to make the easy assumption that the future will resemble the past.

"Stock market getting to you, Farthington?"

31

Big Bang

To observe that stock market swings have become vicious raises no argument. Moves that used to occur over several days or weeks are now compressed into hours. Moreover, the prospects for a return to the "good old days" are rather dim. On the other hand, it is oft forgotten that some of the good old days had their wilder moments, too. For instance, abrupt swings were a characteristic of the stock market of the late '30s in the aftermath of a great bear market. Small investors decided that they had had enough of the stock market. Fewer participants in the market led to more volatility. But looking back, there was more opportunity too.

The biggest players in today's stock market are the institutional investors and the flat-out speculators. Small investors have taken refuge in the bond market or its equivalent. Equities as a percent of total household assets are near the lowest levels in 30 years. While these Federal Reserve statistics don't include the public's holdings of equity mutual funds, neither do they include holdings of bond mutual funds. Furthermore, it is evident from investment industry statistics that there has been a substantial liquidation of the public's equity mutual fund position. The consequences are serious.

Public investors have been the main supporters of small, emerging companies. Most institutional investors are precluded from taking an active interest in these companies because of their small size, scant history, and relatively illiquid markets. When the public withdraws its support en masse, the markets in these stocks not only deteriorate, they become increasingly illiquid, which is to say that it takes less and less trading volume to move these stocks either up or down. Consequently, a large buy or sell order will have a disproportionate effect on a stock's performance. Investors of limited resources don't like being whipsawed, so increased volatility drives more and more of them from the marketplace.

That's the bad news. But change in the marketplace usually cuts both ways. Fewer personal investors means more volatility, and it means more inefficiency, which is the high-flown way of saying bargains among small stocks are increasing. Based upon long-accepted investment yardsticks, some of these companies will offer unusual value. But the odds are that until something develops to provoke a change in small-investor attitudes, these values are not likely to receive the recognition that they deserve. Additionally, an illiquid market means that offerings of new issues and secondary will also dry up, so that opportunities to replenish capital or finance new undertakings in the public market are foreclosed. The consequences might be fatal to an emerging company.

While the price might be right, this is no game for the impatient investor. Nor is macho resignation to increased volatility an answer. What is needed is diligence in searching out severe undervaluations and endurance in seeing commitments through to fruition.

Lesson
Broad changes in investor attitudes can create whole classes of bargains among stocks. However, bargain hunting among out-of-favor stocks requires enduring patience and long-term goals.

"Forget my saying that the earnings of Ever Brighter Tomorrows Inc. couldn't possibly get any worse. I've lowered my estimate."

32

Buck Stop

It's a rare investor who doesn't feel completely lost at times. There are so many conflicting opinions, and facts can be so muddled. Where do you turn? Certainly somebody out there has penetrated the seemingly impenetrable; someone has the right answers and knows precisely what to do. Of course, someone has and does. It's the expert. The more you know about investing in stocks, the more you realize how much more there is to know. So, asking experts for help makes good sense.

The trouble comes when you try to find one. Not that they are few and far between; it just isn't easy to sort them out. You might begin by eliminating the experts you *don't* want.

The worst of the lot is one whose expertise is in telling you what you want to hear. Don't join a fan club. Popularity is a poor clue to good expert judgment. Look instead for expert opinions that are a worthy challenge to your current point of view. Another expert to avoid is the one who has recently achieved notoriety. Never mind that this expert had been consistently wrong before, that's in the past. Stopped clocks are right twice a day, and so, from time to time, are the far-out predictions of some experts. That's not serviceable enough for you.

Then there's the expert who was dramatically correct, but who neglects to tell you that the correctness was accidental. His or her basic assumptions were erroneous, but something unforeseen happened to make a prediction correct. Take the time to explore the basis on which significant predictions were made. Don't expect solid judgments to be built on accidents.

Also beware of the expert hedger who takes both sides of an issue. Valued opinions are rarely rendered without an "on the other hand." Admittedly, it's helpful to see contrasting viewpoints, but the aim is to dispel confusion, not add to it. If an expert is to help, you want the benefit of personal experience and sound judgment.

At the other extreme is the cocksure expert who can find no room for a dissenting opinion. There is a very good chance that bravado is being substituted for weakness in substance. Some experts make good bullies, but that won't help your portfolio performance.

There is a role for the experts, be they brokers, researchers, or advisors. Just be careful not to demand the impossible. No one can divine the future and without that power, mistakes will be made, even with the benefit of long experience and sound judgment. The biggest danger comes from delegating too much and abdicating your commonsense oversight. Regardless of what the experts propose, it's your wealth that is at risk. Take no long shots at the behest of an expert. Remember, that expert is approaching the dice table with your money.

Lesson
Experts can help you. Their professional experience should have beneficially tempered their judgment. But don't set your expectations too high, and never subjugate your own commonsense judgment to the advice of an expert.

"Never mind all the price-earnings stuff. Just put me down for 100 shares of IBM to win, 100 shares of Xerox to place, and 100 shares of AT&T to show."

33

No Show

Equity investing shares something in common with betting, and it's not just a matter of taking chances. Investing and betting both involve calculating the probabilities of winning and losing. At the racetrack, it is no accident that long shots carry high odds. Favorites don't always win, but they perform consistently better than long shots.

Because gambling is a winner-take-all proposition, it's an optimist's game, and the players stoically accept total loss as part of it. Investing in stocks should be neither an optimist's nor a pessimist's game, but only an intellectual exercise. Large losses or a total wipeout doesn't mean bad luck, just that risks were misunderstood or ignored somewhere along the line.

Actually, investors are of two minds toward the risks inherent in the money game. At one extreme, they blithely ignore them, and at the other, they are so anxious to lower them that they needlessly penalize portfolio performance.

Losses are an unavoidable part of investing in stocks. No one likes to think about the unpleasant consequences of being in the market in the wrong way or at the wrong time. But it's a particularly foolish investor who doesn't think occasionally about the price levels where the stocks he or she holds would normally be considered oversold under present circumstances. The comparison of current prices against these bedrock prices provides some measure of peril and at least serves to dispel the debilitating euphoria that always accompanies a "hot" stock or a "hot" market.

Otherwise it's tough to measure downside risk. There are simply too many ways for a stock to sour. Notwithstanding that handicap, you should recognize that there are two kinds of risk in a stock. There is the risk caused by sensitivity to declines in the broad market trend and the risk that is unique to the company's business.

Stock market history demonstrates that downdrafts in the market are by far the most important factor in correctly appraising your downside vulnerability. When the broad market declines, there are few exceptions to the trend. However, there is a further step. You should develop some feeling for whether a specific stock will fall in line with a market decline, or do better or worse than it. Charts of a stock's past price action relative to a popular market index, such as the S&P 500, will give you the insight you need. You should question whether any extra risk exposure is tolerable or is adequately offset by the opportunity.

It is hard to say whether investors suffer most from too little attention to risk or too much. Some investors are very intolerant of losses and take their failures personally. To observe that some losses are inescapable offers no solace. Instead, over time they become more and more risk-averse, forgetting that there is literally no place for an investor to hide. Even cold, hard cash withers under the heat of inflation. There is no substitute for a positive attitude toward risk.

Lesson

Losses may be unavoidable, but unnecessary and completely unanticipated losses are something else again. Being alert to your risks pays. Being immobilized by fear of risk hurts.

"Huntley, are you one of those sophisticated investors that the columnists write about?"

<u>34</u>

Smarts

What is Street savvy? In a nutshell, it might be taken to mean some commonsense rules for making investment judgments that have been gained through experience. It also might imply an innate shrewdness and a particular ability to outsmart and outmaneuver other participants in the market. Investors who lack such talent surely must be at the mercy of those who have it. But are they? The answer is both yes and no.

Start with the obvious. Remember the well-worn taunt, "If you're so smart, why aren't you rich?" If successful investors had only to prey on the uninitiated or less shrewd, the market would have been cornered long ago. The very rich are able to hire the world's best and brightest money managers and thus build even greater fortunes. Yet the record says that these same professionals have a tough time beating the unmanaged performance of the popular averages, let alone being able to amass great wealth at the expense of others. So, while Street savvy counts for something, it is not everything.

Nevertheless, Street savvy is a real dividing line between inexperienced and seasoned investors and ultimately separates inferior performance from superior. Here are four traits that mark a sophisticated investor:

- *Healthy humility.* Streetwise investors are realistic in their expectations. Their anticipations have been shattered so often that "sky's the limit" stocks or invitations to "make a killing" hold little attraction for them. Moreover, they know that fortuitous events destined to drive stocks higher rarely occur on schedule. Most often, they're late, if they occur at all.

- *Leadership.* Canny investors are self-reliant, even though they may lean heavily on the expertness of their peers. They have learned to ignore the blandishments of market gurus and the interpreters of its nuances. They make their own judgments. In contrast, amateurs are bedeviled by the conviction that someone else, somewhere else holds the key to their investment success. They are prepared to follow blindly.

- *Foresight.* Mature investors know that the real payoff comes from how correctly they anticipate pertinent events rather than how they react. Their eyes are on what the future may hold. Neophytes, on the other hand, are hooked on the "news." As a consequence, they follow the news to their disadvantage.

- *Discipline*. Savvy investors control their emotions. Their decisions have intellectual roots. Long ago, they abandoned the search for perfection. If they can approximate reasonable goals, that's good enough. Tyros get bound up in trying to buy at the bottom and sell at the top. If that isn't bad enough, they limit their decisions by eighths and quarters of price.

These seem like significant differences, and they are. Then why aren't the market's beginners grist for the smarties' mill? The answer is that most of what both of them need to know lies in the future and is dimly perceived at best. Nevertheless, Street savvy is something worth acquiring.

Lesson
There is profit in learning from hands-on experience with the often witless antics of the market. Even better is profiting from the experience of others. Above all, practice self-reliance and avoid the siren song of "experts."

"I'm in bed and in my dream a voice says, 'Buy Kodak.' Then another voice says, 'Sell Kodak,' but a third voice says, 'Buy Kodak.' Dammit, two out of three ain't bad odds, so let's buy Kodak."

35

Gotta Hunch?

Plain logic would seem to imply that the more serious homework you do before making an equity commitment, the better your investment performance will be. An enticing idea, but experience shows it to be flawed. There appears to be no limit to the surprises, shocks, and disappointments that companies and their stocks encounter after you are satisfied with your factual research.

And, no matter how diligently you may search for precision, that goal will prove unattainable. You simply can't piece all the innumerable bits of relevant information together. Nor can you know the unknowable, that is, what the future will bring. Many times it takes guesses, hunches, intuition, or whatever you care to call it to bridge the gap. That may sound somewhat reckless, but not necessarily so.

Hunches are their most valuable when they come *after* the homework is done, not before. By themselves, hunches have no more value than an itch. But when tied to something more solid, a hunch can work for you.

This is where past experience can play a key role. For instance, it's a given that superior investment results come both from going with and going against the investor herd. But when? There is no fine line or set of instructions that will tell you when to throw the switch. You will be looking for signs of excess, but how much excess is enough to justify bucking the crowd? Enter intuition.

Over time, you may be able to develop a feeling for the way that a specific stock or industry group behaves. Some, more often than not, will lead or follow a broad market move. It is well known that stocks of companies especially sensitive to the swings of the business cycle usually begin their recovery well before an economic downturn actually ends. Bells don't ring when this occurs, but it can probably be sensed. Also, individual stocks have trading peculiarities. You may not recognize that pattern as such, but if there, it probably has registered in your subconscious mind and can be turned to a profit.

Occasionally a new product will be critical to a company's success. Your gut reaction as to whether it will fly or crash may be as good as that of the company's management. The final judgment is in the marketplace. Remember the Edsel? Many investors bailed out of Ford Motor stock when they got their first look at the car and cashed in on their instincts.

Hunches about the character and competence of a company management should be ignored at your peril. The vast majority of investors will never personally meet a company's senior management to get a firsthand impression. Still, it's imperative to form an opinion. Ask yourself, How well does the management communicate with their shareholders? Do the company news releases and reports seem slippery, insincere, self-serving? There is no litmus test for management capability other than the passage of time. You may not have that kind of time. Trust your instincts.

Lesson

There's more to it than deciding whether the facts make a stock a potential winner or loser. Hunches are impossible to quantify but that doesn't make them any less valuable.

"Ed, I'd like you to meet Fred Simpson, Joe Silverman, and Sally Curtis. Fred's an expert, Joe's a professional, and Sally's a leading authority."

36

On the Other Hand

There are two easy ways to distinguish sophisticated investors from neophytes. First, ask how heavily they rely on experts. Second, inquire whether more investment research would help to improve their returns.

Knowledgeable investors soon limit their dependence on the opinion of experts. They find experts to be about as wrong as anyone else. Consequently, they reason, if mistakes are going to be made, they may as well make them themselves. Inexperienced investors, on the other hand, cling to the naive belief that in the investment arena someone, somewhere, somehow has the guidance they seek. If one expert should disappoint them, they are ready to move on to the next.

Experienced investors, after finding themselves drowning in a sea of research information, eventually learn that it is the quality of their own questions that counts, not the quantity of the answers. In contrast, amateurs are completely convinced that if only they had a little more time each day to spend with *Barron's*, the *Wall Street Journal*, or the business pages they would be more competitive with more experienced investors. They rarely stop to ask what they are looking for other than fewer mistakes and better returns.

This is not to imply that the opinions of experts don't have value. They do. It is simply that stock market experts are not infallible. It is only when you become convinced that you can't begin to know or anticipate everything that will affect the direction of stock prices that humility begins to bear fruit. At that point, your search should turn from being interested in everything to concentrating on what is most important.

Much of Wall Street's expert analytical efforts are directed to the commercial aspects of individual businesses. Research analysts take considerable pride in being able to interview management, dissect income statements and balance sheets, and then forecast a company's future earnings within pennies per share. That these efforts are fraught with failures doesn't seem to deter their efforts. Next, analysts examine industry prospects, hoping to find some common positive or negative threads that will reinforce their judgments about a company. Finally, they may try to address the forces driving the company's stock up and down in the market-place.

It takes real humility to admit that the process should be reversed. Somehow, it is regarded as more befitting for an expert to concentrate on the hard facts surrounding a business rather than the vicissitudes of the marketplace. The truth is that stock prices are driven in the short term by shifts in investor psychology and by individual company earnings trends only in the long term.

Lesson
Humility is the beginning of superior investment performance. Good investment research begins when you recognize limitations, strip down to the essentials, and skip the merely interesting.

"My great aunt Edith appeared to me in a dream last night. She smiled slightly, said, 'Remember the crash—convert to cash,' and disappeared."

37

Ever-Present Value

Following the news of the day leads inexperienced investors down the wrong path again and again. When thoroughly frightened by incessant headlines forecasting economic gloom and doom, they run for cover and unload their equity positions. All the while, their more experienced counterparts are beginning to rebuild their commitments. When buoyed by headlines reporting economic prosperity bursting at the seams, inexperienced investors are in the market with both feet. But their counterparts will ignore temptation and instead use the good fortune to take profits and build reserves for use on another day.

Sophisticated investors never lose sight of something that less experienced investors tend to overlook, i.e., the market is first and foremost a discounter of the future. When much of the business news is announced, they correctly assume that it has already been reflected in the market. To be sure, there are true surprises in the "news," but given the speed of modern communications, these are so swiftly reflected that there is precious little time for most investors to react.

There is an old, but serviceable, market adage that says "sell on the news." Of course, that advice assumes that the "news" is quite good and relatively unanticipated. The converse is also true. Consequently, success in the stock market lies in getting ahead of significant news and following a predetermined plan of action. Acting behind the news is quite frequently a formula for failure. Make it a habit to think about the headlines of the future.

Yet the process is trickier than that. After you have mastered the discipline of ignoring much market news, you will find yourself facing a much thornier challenge, i.e., knowing when to act. Obviously, there is considerable danger in being too early or too late.

Market history makes clear that good timing is the one element most crucial to success. The best part of the profit may lie in the early stages of a market recovery as it shrugs off a deeply oversold condition. The best part of a strong market is at the very end when investors toss caution to the wind in the frantic scramble for capital gains.

The stock market has a tendency to move to extremes. When it begins to look frothy and overvalued, most often it will surprise you and climb still higher. And, even when the market appears oversold and bargains are plentiful, danger still lies ahead.

Train yourself to develop a set of expectations about the trend of the market. That way you can ignore the events that fall within a normal range. It's only the significant deviations from your expectations that should merit your prompt attention.

Lesson

Returns on all stocks lie in the future; all the rest is history. Consequently, the market primarily functions as a discounting mechanism. This all sounds simple enough until you realize that as you try to anticipate the market's trend, you can't know all that you need to know. However, even a faulty set of expectations is better than none at all.

"Now, son, as you pursue this takeover, remember, you may be visited by pride, envy, lust, covetousness, sloth, anger, and gluttony, but go for it!"

<u>38</u>

Nice Guys Last

There is a familiar saying that "nice guys finish last." Some believe that the same may be said of companies. After all, the business of business is supposed to be business—competitive, giving no quarter.

Partly true, at least to the extent that business goals should not be subverted to altruistic goals. Nevertheless, you will find that the more successful companies never lose sight of a responsibility to profit by honestly satisfying wants and needs at a reasonable price.

Be alert for the sleaze factor in the companies whose stocks you own. Insist on true integrity. To do otherwise is not only unnecessary, but downright foolhardy because you are accepting avoidable risk. Unethical managements may gain short-term advantage, but by their actions they are creating ticking time bombs.

In simplest terms, the issue for the investor should be not just bottom-line results, but how they are achieved. How do you spot the bad guys? Here are a few thoughts:

- One of the best sources for a quick integrity check is a company's competitors. If the company has been a bad actor, the word quickly gets around the industry.
- If you have an opportunity to talk to employees in middle management, you may learn that the pronouncements of those up the corporate ladder don't match the word on the firing line. On the other hand, if you find strong loyalty to the company, be encouraged.
- Watch labor relations for signs of trouble. Take frequent strikes as a sign of bad faith in management.
- Ask how well the company gets along with the regulatory agencies in its industry. If conflicts or large fines are reported too often, that's a serious warning, even if guilt is not admitted.
- To detect managements bent on self-enrichment at the shareholders' expense, read the proxy statements for clues.
- What is the company's attitude toward its community responsibilities? Has it established an honorable record or does it act as if it operates in a social vacuum?
- Find out where the company stands on environmental issues, as there may be liabilities from past insensitivities.

- Abuse of accounting niceties is another clue. Time spent with a company's annual report, particularly its fine print, will help you distinguish between "reported" and "true" earnings, regardless of management blandishments.

Business ethics and responsibilities are not the concern solely of philosophers. The aura of bad management can haunt a company and depress its stock for a very long time; ultimately, investors will prove indifferent to even fundamental improvements.

Lesson

Avoid like the plague companies with questionable reputations. As an investor in the stock, you will pay the price—underperformance—for their transgressions.

"Didn't I tell you that if you financed the takeover with junk bonds, the chickens would one day come home to roost?"

39

Roosters

Mismanagement, the investor's curse. When management failures surface, it's usually late in the day. When the bad news breaks, your wisest course is to run for cover. Serious problems are seldom cured overnight. Moreover, the company's competitors are sure to regard the lapses as an invitation to improve their relative position. If the company's problems persist, the stock will most likely under-perform the market and be relegated to "dog" status. If the problems are addressed and corrective steps are taken, the stock may be viewed as a "turn-around" situation.

Investors are advised again and again to avoid "dogs" and "turn-arounds." Labels such as these stick like glue. Nevertheless, market history shows that stocks can quickly shed their "dog" image when they outperform the market for awhile. As for "turn-arounds," infusions of new management has at times been the key to the reversal of a company's misfortunes.

Correctly judging the difference between image and reality opens the door to very substantial returns, but it is not all that easy. There are, however, a few clues that will aid your search. For instance, if a stock declines and then settles into a long, narrow trading range, it may be implied that whatever developments caused the stock to fall are now fully reflected in the stock's price. The omen is clearer if trading volume stays abnormally low. One important caveat. Stocks that have fallen too far from favor will have few friends. Consequently, if the entire market should suffer a severe decline, you can expect a "dog" to move to an even lower level. On the other hand, it follows that sharp market declines should be treated as an opportunity to intensify the search for a mismatch between a stock's poor image and the realities of its business.

Stocks fallen from favor will rarely respond to an improved per-spective for the company. Once stung, investors will usually demand an improvement in the company's earnings trend before they will afford it significant attention. Under pressure, many troubled companies will cut prices and mount a vigorous sales campaign. That may create the appearance of progress, but it's false. Such companies are to be avoided. Others will review the company's operations and assets with a view to downsizing the company to current realities. Shun these companies for the time being. Cost-cutting measures take time to materialize at the bottom line.

A bargain hunter should also wonder why misfortune had to strike before management took corrective action. Be especially sensitive to overly defensive explanations by management to their shareholders. Missteps and faulty judgments are an everyday business risk, but they are no excuse for management to be self-serving.

Lesson

If your timing is right, "dogs" and "turn-arounds" can be real money-makers. However, don't jump in too early. Remember that the normal skepticism of other investors toward a fallen stock works for you while you search for further proof. Investors rarely will respond strongly to the first evidence of an earnings reversal.

"Do you remember if lower prices clear the market or clog the market?"

40

Forgotten Law

For sophisticated investors, the name of the game is "value." If a potential investment offers much greater intrinsic value than its current price, then it's rated a "buy." Alternatively, if the current intrinsic value is substantially less than its current price, it's a "sell." Obviously, it's when investors try to measure value that they find the fly in the ointment. But suppose that all investors could accurately measure "value." Wouldn't eliminating undervaluations and overvaluations iron out the swings in the market? The answer is no—for several well-known reasons.

For one, investors have different time horizons in mind when they invest. There is an enormous gulf between speculators and long-term investors. Speculators are relatively unconcerned with value concepts and very sensitive to the news of the moment.

Another reason is that investors differ in their expectations of returns—sort of a greed factor. Finally, investors vary widely in their appetite for taking risk. For some, "blue chips" are the only way to go, while others are only satisfied when they are investing on entrepreneurial frontiers. However, even if all of these differences were adjusted in the prices of stocks, there would remain yet another major force, the one most often neglected when trying to fathom the trend of the market.

With the total value of the stock market fluctuating because of shifting prices, it is hard to isolate the effect of new money being added to, or old money being withdrawn from, the market. Nevertheless, if the supply of shares is constant, additional demand will translate into higher stock prices even though underlying values remain the same. Obviously, higher prices will be needed to convert potential sellers into actual sellers. And vice versa.

Powerful as this force may be, there is no easy method to measure the net effect of shifts in supply and demand. There are many elements, their force is not constant, and they may at times counteract one another. Yet they are so important that it's prudent to keep a weather eye open for some of the more important signs.

For example, the movement from cash equivalent reserves to stock commitments is a potent force. A strong market move creates a strong temptation to join the crowd, particularly near the peak. When the uptrend is broken, there is usually a rush to rebuild reserves, which then further weakens the market. The converse is true for a weak market. You will find it helpful to watch the monthly reports of the net buying or selling of common stock mutual funds. Massive purchases or withdrawals should strengthen the case for a contrary opinion.

When you notice that the supply of new and secondary issues is expanding sharply, be forewarned. Underwriters are skilled at estimating investor demand, but too often they overshoot the mark and create too much supply. The digestion period that follows while the excess supply is absorbed can be painful.

On the downside, watch for a rash of company announcements of authorizations to buy back their stock in the public market. If enough companies are doing that, you can generally assume that managements are reflecting a view that stocks have fallen too far. Buy-backs decrease the supply of stock and leverage demand.

Remember that equity supply and demand forces are global. When institutional portfolio managers switch their preferences from domestic to foreign markets, the impact can be significant. A clue is found in currency exchange rates. Strengthening currencies encourage international investors, weakening currencies discourage.

Lesson
The forces of supply and demand are frequently ignored, yet they impact the trend of the market in significant ways. Watch for evidence of big shifts.

"And now, without further ado or a dry eye in the house, let's raise the curtain and watch short-term interest rates move dramatically lower."

41

That's Entertainment

Stocks react to the announcement of unusually good developments for a company in either of two ways. Sometimes stocks will rise sharply after the announcement, which can be taken as an indication that the company's insiders are well disciplined and that its internal controls on inside information are effective. The good news comes as a true surprise to the investors, and the stock is bid up.

Most often, stocks will sink on a good news announcement. There are usually two reasons for this. The first is that the company's internal controls are not effective, and stock purchases are being made in anticipation of a news release. Sometimes there's been a purposeful leak of the news to research analysts who follow the company and who in turn inform their brokerage firms' most-valued clients. Either way, the news is already discounted by the time the announcement is actually made. So the stock has a tendency to sink on profit taking at the expense of investors reacting to what they *think* is news, but which really isn't.

The second reason that stocks fall on good news is that it attracts the attention of speculators and traders who act on the old adage, "sell on the news." They would rather join the insiders taking their profits than hope that later on eager buyers will ensure their profit at still-higher levels.

It is wise to exercise caution when reacting to good corporate news. Sometimes company managements see in good news an opportunity to set the stage for additional equity financing, particularly if the stock has been turning in a strong performance. When investors find out about the pending earnings dilution from more shares outstanding, their euphoria is quickly dissipated. But company managements and their underwriters are more sanguine because the price decline has taken place from a higher level.

Sometimes good news represents an attempt on the part of management to bestir their laggard stock. A stock split in an uninteresting company without strongly improving fundamentals simply invites stockholders to reexamine the reasons they continue to hold it in their portfolios. Dividend increases that are not soundly justified call payment of the entire dividend into question. Make it a habit to ask yourself what's behind the good news. A little cynical reflection may reveal manufactured or contrived news.

Lesson

Corporate good news can create a dangerous euphoria. Even the most stimulating news fades quickly in investor memory. Consequently, even if you are tempted to add to your present holdings on the strength of good news, there is wisdom in exercising restraint. Use the next dip in the market to make your acquisition at more advantageous price. Your batting average won't be perfect, but it will be better than it would be if you continually chase the news.

"...and to sweeten the deal, J. T., the board is prepared to offer you a salary in the 10-figure range."

42

Among Friends

The role of the company director is to represent the interest of all stockholders. In effect, the board of directors acts as a check on the company's management, even though company officers themselves are usually board members. It is even common that the company's most senior official will be board chair.

When examining the makeup of the board, the first step is to determine how many directors come from the company and how many come from outside the company. When you find that the preponderance of the directors are from the company, be suspicious as to whether the board of directors is independent enough to act on the behalf of the stockholders by resisting undue pressure from the company. The withholding or tempering of bad news is a temptation that too many corporate managers find hard to resist. A strong dissent by outside directors is the best antidote.

Examine the credentials of the outside directors carefully. If they are not particularly distinguished, you can assume that these directors were chosen as management's "good buddies." Their function is limited to being rubber stamps. At the other extreme are the directors who enjoy high public visibility and participate on many boards. Their value is likely limited to "window dressing." The ideal director is someone who can bring skills, contacts, wisdom, and experience to the board. These qualifications are especially important to younger companies.

Many times the mere size of the board of directors offers worthy intelligence. For instance, if the board is small, there is a likelihood that the outside directors were carefully chosen for their cooperative attitude toward management preferences. On the other hand, a large board is probably too unwieldy to support much independence on the part of the outside directors. The pitfalls of a large committee are well recognized.

The company's annual proxy statement will reveal the extent of each individual director's stock ownership and stock options in the company. If a director has a limited financial stake in the company's future, it is essential that there be some substantial offset such as business experience valuable to the company to justify his or her membership on the board. Token holdings of stock are a meaningless gesture. It is reassuring to know that a director's and a shareholder's financial interests are on the same path.

Few investors are in a position to attend the annual meetings of the companies whose shares they hold. Yet it is the best opportunity to size up a company's management and its board of directors. Some companies take the opportunity to carefully report on their stewardship and their aspirations for the company's future. Verbal exchanges with shareholders are open and welcome. Some companies regard their annual meetings as an unwelcome burden and a waste of management's time. Their meetings are perfunctory and stockholder opinions and criticisms are not invited. In reality, these are private companies masquerading as public ones. The shareholder is an outsider and participates in the company's future at his or her peril.

Lesson
Do not overlook the composition of the company's board of directors as a valuable bit of intelligence. Be especially careful of a public company being run as a private preserve.

"Sure, our previous stock market predictions have crashed, but now we've doubled the speed."

43

Number-Numb

Numbers are the shorthand of commerce. In fact, numbers are so much the heartbeat of the investment world that there is an overwhelming desire to measure something—just about anything, in any fashion. Unfortunately, the very utility of numbers tends to obscure the meanings the shorthand is intended to convey.

To illustrate, take a reasonably straightforward concept. Start with the top line, a company's revenues for some period of time. That number is shorthand for the sale of the company's numerous goods and services, but which ones and how are they changing with respect to some previous period of time is not revealed. Most companies won't say, except in the very broadest of terms.

For simplicity's sake, let's assume that the ranking of the company's sales of assorted goods and services is constant. This hypothetical company announces that sales for the just-completed quarter are up 20 percent. Break out the champagne. But wait. In the previous quarter, this hypothetical company reported a top-line revenue decline of 20 percent, so it appears that for six months revenues have shown no change. However, if the hypothetical company started with $100 million in sales, lost 20 percent (which took sales to $80 million), then increased sales 20 percent, the result is sales of $96 million. Sales for the six months would be off by $4 million. Percentage changes are a useful interpretation of what the numbers may hold, but, as illustrated, they are potentially misleading.

Now take this thought and expand it to cover the entire national economy. The top line becomes the gross domestic product (GDP), that is, the total value of all goods and services produced nationally. The concept is enough to boggle the mind when you think of the underlying elements. Imagine yourself flying over the country's major cities and out your window you see countless homes, factories, and shopping centers. Then there are all the economic activities that you don't see on your flight. But worry not. It's all summed up nicely in that familiar economic statistic, the GDP, and reported with a solemnity that suggests that the numbers have been cut in stone.

Certainly, Wall Street reacts as if they had. If the GDP is reported lower than the expectations of the pundits, recession fears surface. If higher than anticipated, the fear of inflation is ignited. The stock market swings on the news. Never mind that some time later the government may significantly revise its GDP numbers. It's old news then.

The sheer volume of national economic data is such a gaggle that long ago there was an attempt to find measurements that would provide some clue as to the future track of the economy. These have become known as the leading, coincident, and lagging economic indicators. Their forecasting accuracy has been notoriously poor. That doesn't seem to dissuade Wall Street's prophets. They are ever at the ready to forecast and analyze a boundless array of indicators ranging from price indices to automobile sales. Every few days, some statistic from the nation's capital becomes grist for their mill.

Admittedly, investors need an economic sense of direction. Unfortunately, over time, the raw estimates and fragmentary samplings commonly employed have taken on a precision that was never anticipated. The frailty of it all is revealed in the wide range of expert forecasts. If the experts all work from the same set of facts, why all the differences?

Lesson

It's a numbers jungle out there. Remember that the numbers used in investment work are only shorthand and have the limitations of shorthand. Try to concentrate on a sense of what the numbers reveal and ignore any pretensions of precision. Be especially careful of information reported as a percentage change.

"No, Mr. Fondley, it is not industry practice to forgive your margin debt as you forgive your debtors."

44

Debtor's Prism

Before you find yourself bound up in the odds of winning or losing, focus on your ultimate investment objective. That may sound complicated, but for the investor there are only two possible objectives. Either you aim to preserve your investment capital or you strive to increase it. If the former, you will want to become more familiar with the various instruments of indebtedness. Whether the paper is a certificate of deposit or a long-term first mortgage, the principles are much the same. You want to rent your savings at a reasonable rate and be assured of their return when due back. Would that it were that simple.

Common sense suggests that the longer you must wait for the repayment of your money, the greater the risk, and therefore the greater should be the rent, i.e., the interest rate. In fact, that pattern prevailed in the bond markets for quite some time, but then superinflation came along. There was even a period when the return from bonds was less than the inflation rate. That meant that, adjusted for inflation, lenders were losing money on their loans. Worse than that, when the loans were repaid, their relative buying power had seriously deteriorated.

As a consequence, lenders began to pay close attention to their "real" return after compensating for the estimated rate of inflation during the length of the loan. Lenders also began to refuse to make long-term loans, so borrowers found themselves paying historically high interest rates for very short term loans. What that means is that whenever the threat of inflation materializes, short-term rates will rise sharply, probably to levels higher than long-term rates. But when the inflation rate cools, the converse will be true. The alert investor would be wise to make compensatory portfolio adjustments in bond maturities.

High inflation brings out another hazard for bondholders when business failures multiply. Too many businesses fail to handle their debt well. If they find themselves unable to increase prices for their goods and services to cope with inflationary pressures, debt will likely do them in. Numerous investment advisory services address the challenge of determining the quality grade of debt instruments, but in times of considerable economic stress, the savvy bond investor expects the unexpected and prepares for the worst by shortening maturities and increasing the quality of holdings. High interest rates can be an alluring trap. Remember that there are few free gifts in the bond market. Interest rates are set high for good and sufficient reason; they are not an exercise in blind generosity.

Sometimes inexperienced investors become so mesmerized with the high quality of a bond, such as a U.S. government security, that they overlook its potential for falling dramatically in current value. After all, the return on every marketable bond must reflect current interest rates. When interest rates rise, bond prices must decline in order to generate a competitive rate.

Federal, state, and local income taxes introduce yet another complication for the bond buyer. Income on certain bonds, usually those issued by states and municipalities, are wholly or partially free from taxes. However, tax-free bonds do not automatically guarantee a superior return. Always calculate the after-tax return on a taxable bond to determine its relative attractiveness.

Lesson
Investing your savings in debt instruments may appear safe and conservative to you, but the volatility of the debt market over the past decade is enough to destroy anyone's peace of mind. Bonds as an alternative to stocks have their uses, but they do not represent a "free lunch."

"Martin and Beane. Broker dealers since 1922. Sanford B. Stokely III, Top Gun of the Week."

45

Fast Track

There's an old saying that in the land of the blind the one-eyed man is king. If ever there was a land of the blind, it's the land of investors. Because all investment returns lie in the future, investors are natural victims on unforeseen events. It doesn't take too many investment disasters before you're convinced of your blindness and ready to pledge allegiance to the one-eyed king. Be aware that there are more than a few pretenders to that throne.

Remember the advertising campaign that featured the headline, "If you've got it, flaunt it"? The sellers of investment have taken that advice to heart. Their track records are prominently displayed for all to admire. However, while investors may be blind, they are not stupid. They want to know how the results were achieved. The responses are often as colorful as the claims.

Most of the one-eyed kings will simply refer you to their professional credentials. That's a good and logical reply. Training and experience should count for something, particularly if mistakes in judgment have been a tempering influence. Unfortunately, that response doesn't indicate whether the track record was a product of deliberate planning or a freak of circumstance, such as a rise in the market due to unpredicted events. Putting the best face on one's track record is understandable, but is the record representative?

Some of the other responses are more specious. There are one-eyed kings who claim to be smarter than the pack. That claim takes more than a little chutzpa and never holds up. Then there are those who claim to be quicker than most in their reactions. These six-shooter cowboys will fire on anything that moves, but how many hits are made when the targets are poorly seen, half-understood, or based on wild rumors? Then there is the claim by some that they can see what others miss. Sometimes a true picture is distorted, but how often and for how long? Still others base their claim to fame on broader and deeper research. They may even avidly solicit inside information about a particular company. However, richness of detail doesn't correlate well with superior investment judgments. It's getting the big perspective correct that counts. Others stake their claim to uniqueness by concentrating on a specific business activity such as retail trade, energy, natural resources, etc. While specialization does help to some extent, it brings the real risk of losing sight of more fundamental forces at work.

Regardless of the rationalizations offered, all the one-eyed kings have something in common. Since all investment returns lie in the future, all are saying or implying that their vision of those future events that will have an impact on security valuations is superior to yours. Given the sheer number and variability of these events, the claim should invite your deepest skepticism.

Lesson

Hot track records do exist, but they are maddeningly difficult to extend. It's not investment results per se that count, but rather a thorough understanding of how they were achieved. Beware of bravado and braggadocio. True professionals are humble in light of the challenges they face.

"After six quarters of outperforming the S&P 500, I'm fired because my record is too good to hold up."

46

Hobgoblin

When investment managers refer to the "good old days," they are probably thinking about the time before investment performance statistics became de rigueur in their profession. Performance consisted of valuing the portfolio and then looking at the bottom line to determine if the client's net worth had risen or fallen. It was after the introduction of the computer that "relative" investment performance became their nemesis. The question uppermost in the client's mind went from "How am I doing?" to "Am I doing as well as I should?"

That this transition was happening in the midst of a great bull market didn't help at all. Greed was in the ascendancy. That a great bear market followed made matters worse. Unbridled fear replaced greed. The net effect was a dramatic shortening of investment time horizons and a focus on detail instead of the larger perspective. It quickly became obvious that performance had to be measured against something. For equity performance, what could be handier than the popular and universally respected Dow Jones Industrials and Standard & Poor's 500 Composite indices? Because of the way they were constructed and because of the companies they represented, few questioned whether these indices had limitations. They became the standards to beat.

Gradually, as the data accumulated, it became clear that the performance of these standards was extraordinarily difficult to surpass. For dedicated and sincere portfolio managers, the revelation was humiliating. Portfolio turnover was increased dramatically in an effort to bolster performance, but that proved counterproductive.

When the limitations of the performance standards became evident, the response was more standards, but even so the search for a more perfect standard proved ephemeral. It should have occurred to clients and investment professionals alike that the dog was chasing its own tail. But it was too late. Performance measurement, however imperfect, was now a permanent fixture.

The clients became scorekeepers and embraced the treasure trove of new statistics with the fervor of sports addicts. Investment managers became mere players in the game. If they didn't measure up, they were fired and replaced. Eventually it was reasoned that if the performances of the standards were consistently better than those of the mass of portfolio managers, why not replace the managers with unmanaged portfolios that as closely as possible resembled the standards?

It's hard to think of another profession where the history of successes and failures is kept with such intensity and precision. Yet the imprecision of the measurement process goes unrecognized. There is no real intelligence in performance measured over a quarter, or six months, or even a year. Experience teaches that the best investment results come from establishing long time horizons and then having the patience to reach them.

Lesson
Reviewing past performance is a legitimate investment exercise, but one that should invite a certain amount of restraint in its application. The client's reasonable objective should determine the appropriate performance standard, the measurement period, and the applicable risk constraints. In investment performance, one size does not fit all.

*"...so that the stocks you hold, Mrs. Parsons, considering the present
market climate, are positioned relative to movement worldwide, which,
as you know, can fluctuate periodically according to shifting economic
trends found both here and..."*

47

Just Browsing

Successful common stock investing involves a bit of a paradox. On
the one hand, the investor should limit his or her interest to those
stocks that promise a well-above-average return. There are so

many ways for risks to materialize that the potential for a well-above-average return is an indispensable offset. Merely "good" stocks have an unfortunate way of becoming "poor" stocks. On the other hand, the search for such returns leaves the undisciplined investor exposed to appeals to base instincts such as unfettered greed.

The best defense is self-discipline. Make investment decisions the product of an intellectual process. Above all, be realistic. Don't be overwhelmed by an enticing story. The size of a potential gain should not blind you to the risks. The secret of investment success is not high opportunity matched by even higher risk. It's curious, but experienced and inexperienced investors alike make the same mistake in their quest for above-average profits. They ignore the time horizon required for commercial developments to unfold. Most investors grasp the implications of portentous developments quickly enough, but they rarely appreciate how long it takes for them to materialize.

Suppose that a pharmaceutical company develops an unusual cancer-fighting drug that has no competition and whose market may be numbered in the billions of dollars. But, even if the drug eventually proves successful, its impact on the company's earnings is five years away. The key question is not the dimensions of the opportunity but whether it is already fully reflected in the price of the company's stock. Being in on the ground floor for such a momentous opportunity makes five years seem like the twinkle of an eye. But it isn't, at least not as measured by the daily churning of the market. If the company will be reporting red ink for much of that time, then almost certainly the market's occasional bellyaches will present opportunities to buy the stock at more realistic prices, great science notwithstanding.

You do not want to underestimate the usefulness of your broker. Not only should you be shown and informed of investment merchandise of potential interest, but recognize, in your own self-interest, that most would-be investors need the salesperson's push to turn thought into action. However, it is no disservice to your broker to check the amount of sales commission on underwritings and distributions on either the stock exchange or the over-the-counter market being offered to you. Sometimes, in order to move a block of an unpopular or obscure stock, the sales commission is made much larger than usual. That's intended to inspire the sales efforts, but sometimes that temptation leads to contacting clients who should otherwise not be considered as good prospects for the offering.

Lesson

Be wary of anything that hints of inside information about to be made public or a short-lived opportunity. The stock market is rarely that kind to the uninitiated. After you have suffered through enough failed hot tips or once-in-a-lifetime opportunities, you will learn how to insulate yourself from such appeals and save yourself that agony.

"Of course, our analyst is firm on his earnings estimate."

<u>48</u>

Sure Thing

Even if we admit that there is no such thing as a "sure bet," why should some stocks that look like almost certain winners suddenly become pathetic losers? Performance was fine until you made your commitment, then things began to go wrong. The probabilities are that the warning signs were there, but you didn't recognize them or you chose to ignore them.

It's a rare hot stock that doesn't cool down, but there is a variety of reasons for the change—beyond the obvious one that the stock's price was far exceeding its fundamental value. While it is easier by far to buy a stock that is rising, ultimately you will have to contend with the early birds in the stock who will want to sell and take profits. If the stock's price action is too frothy, look for the short sellers to come in.

Even the best "story" wears thin after it has been told often enough. Unless some development comes along to refresh the story, you can assume that the stock will fall. And then there is always competition from the next hot story, which converts your "story" stock into a source of funds.

Another common source of sure bets is the "hot" initial public offering. The pricing of new offerings is a dicey affair. Most often, price is determined by comparison with the price of similar companies. But the comparison may be weak. Even so, the underwriters will have a range of offering prices in mind. In the initial stages, there is a testing of the waters that divines investor receptivity of the deal. If receptivity seems warm, the offering price will be moved to the high end of the range. If cool, the opposite. Also, the size of the offering has some flexibility. The underwriting agreement usually has a clause, called a "green shoe" in the trade, that in the event of exceptional demand authorizes additional shares for distribution. If demand proves extraordinary, the company may be asked to enlarge the offering and the prospectus will be amended accordingly. In either event, beware making a commitment. A higher price plus a substantial increase in the shares offered has cooled many an otherwise hot offering.

When an underwriting becomes hot, another factor comes into play. As word of the deal circulates, demand turns to a clamor for shares from "riders" who have no interest in the company as an investment but only seek a quick profit. Consequently, they are the first to sell if the stock does not immediately move to a premium over the offering price. That liquidation can break the back of the offering and lead to a downward spiral.

The worst of the sure bets is one based on an inside tip. Even if the tip comes from an unimpeachable source, ask yourself how many others might have been made privy, as you have been, to the information. The point is that the tip may already be reflected in the stock's price. Also, recognize that even the best inside information has a way of going sour. For example, firm agreements can come unglued and earnings about to be reported can be significantly altered.

Lesson
The ways for a "sure thing" to go wrong are legion. Diversification is your only protection against the unknown.

"Dear Shareholder: In an effort to reduce an overstocked inventory, you will be receiving under separate cover a number of the company's household products of equal or greater value than your regular quarterly dividend."

<u>49</u>

A Tale of Two

There are many ways for companies that appear to be alike to be quite different. Some of the worst delusions in the stock market stem from the uncritical use of earnings comparisons. The flaw is the implied assumption that earnings are as comparable as prices. However, the earnings of companies can differ so much in quality that it is like claiming that fresh bread and stale bread are no different because they look alike.

For example, assume that two companies each report the same earnings, dividends, sales growth, research and development expenditures, etc., but that they show sharply different trends in their receivables and inventories. Further assume that the first company has held its receivables and inventories in roughly the same relationship to its sales in previous years. On the other hand, assume that the second company has been building inventory which it hopes to sell through easier credit terms. Is this a significant difference? Yes, because the second company has much more exposure to an unexpected business downturn. But can an investor assume that the first company will turn in a superior investment performance? If the second company is forced into liquidating its inventory through much deeper discounts, the first company will have little alternative except to meet the price cuts and temporarily endure the near-term, negative impact on its reported earnings—judicious planning notwithstanding.

But think of a different scenario. Suppose that the second company correctly surmised that an upturn in the economy was close at hand. Now they have all the advantage of being able to respond to increased demand from the market place. Under these circumstances, the more prudently managed company would suffer both in its business and in its appeal for investors. While the facts are known, only time will tell which is the superior investment.

Another illustration. Suppose that two like companies in the same industry report identical earnings. However, one has spent heavily on new product development and the other spends little on the assumption that its products have achieved commodity status so that further R&D is likely to prove unproductive. Note that even if the research expenditures of the first company proved

147

totally unproductive, the mere cessation of these expenditures would immediately improve earnings. Besides, what a world of difference there would be if the R&D of the first company proved productive.

And another scenario. Companies doing business multinationally frequently have their earnings altered by currency translations. What may appear as impressive jumps in foreign revenues may not find their way to the bottom line. Or foreign profits may get an unexpected boost from a relatively strong U.S. dollar. Currency translations can bring either opportunity or risk, so it's wise to recognize how much of one company's revenues and earnings versus another company's are concentrated overseas.

These distinctions in the quality of earnings are important. Unfortunately, unless you have the skills to uncover them you must rely on the judgment of trained security analysts.

Lesson

Just because share prices of individual stocks are directly comparable, it should not be inferred that the same applies to per share earnings of seemingly similar companies. This caveat may seem obvious, but frequently security analysts will compare price-earnings ratios of several stocks without adjusting for earnings quality. Investors are thus led into a trap.

"Then my broker called to say that his last rumor was rumored to be false."

50

Now Hear This

It's not bad enough that investors find themselves drowning in facts, figures, and verbiage, they must also contend with rumors, half-truths, and falsehoods. That might imply that deception is rampant in the investment world. It may be, but it is the natural product of too much uncertainty. The easiest solution would be to ignore the problem altogether, but that involves some peril— ignorance is not bliss in the stock market.

There is an understandable tendency to want to know everything you can about the companies whose stock you own. The idea is "Better informed is better prepared." But better informed might also mean better distracted from the attainment of your objectives. Your aim should be to cut the information problem down to size. You can start by insisting to your broker or advisor that your interest is limited to the basics, i.e., what makes your investment more or less valuable. That may cut you out of the loop for an occasional scoop, but you will find that fewer such distractions will mean fewer mistakes in judgment. As some comfort, you can also bet that whenever you hear a rumor, you will be late in hearing it. Wall Street professionals transmit information with such incredible speed that by the time you are informed, the information most likely has already been taken into account by the market, whatever its relevance may be.

Wall Street rumors titillate like any piece of gossip or hearsay, so when you hear them, practice some self-discipline. Try to distinguish between rumors about a company's business and rumors about something that could influence the performance of its stock. You can make this distinction by asking if the company's fundamental value is affected. Rumors about new products, new markets, and competitive developments can be helpful at times.

The worth of rumors that might affect the stock's performance are much harder to judge. For instance, suppose that one of your companies is rumored ready to announce additional equity financing. More stock outstanding should translate into lower earnings per share and price weakness. But an underwriting is also an opportunity for a company to tell its story to many potential investors. How will the funds raised be applied? That might represent a major new opportunity for the company. Take another example. You might be told that a major institutional holder of your stock has just liquidated its position. Bad news? Maybe, but you don't know. The decision might have been made for reasons unrelated to the company's future worth, or it might be a mistake in judgment. Keep in mind that many factors influence a stock's price performance, and rumors usually concern but one small aspect.

There are rumors that contain an element of truth and rumors that are downright false. While it is illegal to plant a false rumor, it nevertheless does happen from time to time. The leverage provided by the options market is a powerful temptation for some to attempt to manipulate the price of the underlying stock. Be aware.

Rumors that titillate can be tolerated, but they should be recognized as costly distractions. Rumors meant to galvanize you to take action are the most suspect. "Act now or face the consequences" is a common appeal. Long-term investors insulate themselves from this lure.

Lesson

The investor's problem is the pertinence and quality of investment information, not its scarcity. Avoid the distractions caused by too much attention to daily business developments. The purveyors of investment information would like to convince you otherwise, but don't become a financial news glutton.

"Mr. Bergerhoff, some very attractive investment opportunities are floating around out here. I think you better come take a look."

51

Winner's Circle

Year after year, the stock market records events that should be the cause for great celebration, but many times these events pass completely unnoticed. Year after year, there are stocks that sometime during that year reached a price level that distinguished them as true superachievers. Their prices rose from being worth the equivalent of $1 per share to $100 per share. Said in a little more enticing form that means that if you had originally invested $10,000 in one of these stocks and then waited patiently for your reward, your investment would be worth a million dollars. Obviously, that doesn't happen overnight.

It might be assumed that these stocks were initially hidden treasure and only discoverable by a privileged few early on in their development. On the contrary, these superperformers are usually anything but obscure. When the market presented these milliondollar opportunities, they were already well-recognized names like General Motors, Sears Roebuck, IBM, Eastman Kodak, etc. You didn't have to buy IBM when very few investors knew of the company's existence. In fact, it was possible to seize a million-dollar opportunity in IBM when the company had already achieved considerable stature in the business world and when institutional investors were already putting the stock into their portfolios for the long haul.

As an investor, you didn't have to be in on the ground floor of the automobile, the airplane, the telephone, or the computer to obtain vastly superior returns on your capital. In fact, it helped to stand back in the formative years. There was no unusual penalty in making your commitment when the opportunity was better defined. The point is that even today such opportunities are present. There are well-recognized companies positioned now for future supergrowth. But don't wait for your broker to call with one of these stellar ideas. Look around at what is happening. There has been a literal explosion in the world's technology base. What was impossible a few short years ago is today not only possible, but economical as well. The scramble to commercialize this new knowledge is intense. By hindsight at very least, you will discover what you missed when you see which of these supercompanies found great opportunity in great change.

The challenge is to exercise your foresight. It is too easy to be caught up in what is happening now. Recognize that many commercial opportunities cast their shadow before them. After all, even the best opportunity can be exploited only so fast. The trick is to avoid near-term distractions and to improve the quality of your vision with practice.

There is most often a trade-off between the assurance of a bright future and the high price of the stock you want to buy. This means that a superpotential stock seldom comes cheaply. What you can see, other investors can also see. However, there is a big difference between investors in the courage to act. After courage comes patience. It takes superpatience to endure all the way to the ultimate payoff in the face of countless provocations to take profits or switch to a "real mover."

Lesson
Be demanding in your stock selections. Remember that committing to a superwinner takes courageous action and enduring patience.

"Oh, that's the pile of money Artie made in the stock market last year."

52

Unprofitable Experience

Profits are what investing in the stock market is all about. The more, the merrier. In fact, you will often hear it said that "you can't go wrong taking a profit." That sounds sensible, as far as it goes. But suppose that the stock you sold was a potential super-winner. Maybe you should have been told to "cry all the way to the bank" instead. Think how easy it is to go wrong. You've picked a superwinner, and then the stock takes off. The temptation to cash in on your good fortune proves irresistible, so you sell. Then your superwinner reflects its strong fundamentals and continues its upward course. What do you do? Well, unless you are endowed with rare courage, you will settle back contentedly with your nice profit and hunt for another superwinner. Years later you can sob over "what might have been."

It is hardly revelation to observe that the secret to a successful "buy and hold" strategy is to buy right in the first place. Logical as that may seem, you will discover most investors are less concerned with "buying right" than with being able to exit quickly with a profit or to correct their "mistakes" in an instance. Ask yourself how many shareholders in a superstock like Merck or IBM stayed the entire course and pocketed a million. You can bet that a much larger number owned the stock briefly. Sadder still are the traders who were in and out of the stock, sometimes winning and sometimes losing, but never realizing the substantial capital gains that simple patience would have generated.

One of the most successful promotional campaigns for a mutual fund was built around the rhetorical question, "Do you sincerely want to be rich?" Most of us would settle for being rich, sincere or otherwise. But obviously that question touched a responsive chord because the campaign was wildly successful in corralling new investors. It was as if investors were willing to declare, at least sub-liminally, their serious intent to invest their savings for the long haul. However, experience teaches that such good resolve quickly dissipates in the occasional storms that plague the market.

When you have been fortunate enough to own a stellar stock, you will often be advised to "skim off some of the cream," that is, to salt away some of the profit. Advisors will recite that tired Wall

Street adage "Bulls and bears make money in the market, but hogs never do." Recognize, however, that the issue is rarely greed. What usually is being voiced is concern over the near-term prospects for the market rather than the long-term prospects for the company. The cart has been put in front of the horse. And, even if the advice is correct, positions in a superwinner are seldom restored to their original level. Some other recommendation always seems to intervene.

Too little consideration is given to the impact of taxes on the decision to take a profit in a stock. It should be obvious that taxes paid leave less money committed to the next investment decision. But, that observation aside, it is even more pertinent to observe that tax considerations cannot become the tail that wags the investment dog. Many a substantial profit has evaporated in the decision to avoid taxes by doing nothing.

Lesson

Be wary of advice to take a profit in a company with strong fundamentals. Make sure that the advice addresses the future course of the company and not the future course of the stock market.

"Miss Chambers, bring me some pertinent facts, revealing statistics, and current data."

53

Everything?

The search for a winning stock usually begins with a scramble for the pertinent facts and numbers. That's admirable enough, but it's too easy to get lost in the swamp of detail.

Keep in mind the three requisites for attaining vastly superior returns from stocks. First, you must have the vision to see what other investors also see, but in a different light, or see what other investors fail to see. Second, your research should be so complete that it inspires the courage to act on your vision. Third, your conviction must be so strong that you will freeze your resolve to stay the course, no matter the temporary distractions.

Investment vision has so many aspects that it is near impossible to define, but change is the common denominator. You must be able to envision a stock as being much more attractive at some time in the future than it is today. Sometimes all that is required is the passage of time to convert disbelievers of the company's story into enthusiasts. Sometimes the vision is fuzzy. Stocks develop reputations, some of which are deserved and some otherwise. When a company with a poor record undergoes real change, the investment crowd usually misses the event. How that change occurs is what makes investing so very interesting.

Many investors naively convince themselves that executing a "buy" decision requires little effort. They watch a high-performance stock take off and in a wink convince themselves that they would have had the intellectual self-discipline to buy such a wonderful stock had they just known about it. In real life, the "buy" decisions are much harder to make and usually require some outside arm twisting. It is almost axiomatic that extraordinary opportunities demand unusual courage if research is to be converted into action.

Reason will suggest that it is easy to hold onto a winner. It's a logical expectation that investors will tend to fall in love with stocks that have been exceptionally profitable. However, practice shows otherwise. It takes strong resolve to forgo the temptation to bank a big profit. After all, at any given time there is no lack of contrary opinions either about an individual stock, the stock market, or the economy. These opinions exert an enormous tug to salt away a big profit. Not only will economic and business developments impinge on your peace of mind, but your advisors will contribute their fair share of distraction. The main thrust on Wall Street is to encourage investors to active participation in the stock market. Prepare to be persuaded to buy and sell frequently by well-crafted siren songs filled with vision, facts, and figures.

Lesson
Investors buying the same stock at the same price and at the same time have different visions, courage, and patience. Turn this difference to your advantage.

"Make mine a 'hot' stock any day."

54
Ain't Easy

Let's take some inspiration from some of the market's onetime wallflowers that later went on to become the queens of the ball. PepsiCo Inc., which qualifies as an all-time superstock, was at one point in its history a true wallflower. Can you believe that this stock languished in stock market limbo for seven years? More to the point, can you imagine the temptation to kiss off this loser sometime during those seven years? But, if you had invested $10,000 at any time during the flat spot, your $10,000 would eventually have grown to be worth more than a million. This illustration suggests that patience may even take precedence over timing as a first principle. Moreover, if you think that this opportunity was a rare exception, consider that Sharpe & Dome (later merged with Merck) could have been purchased at prices that would have ultimately made a patient investor of $10,000, any time during a 12-year period, a millionaire.

But how do you avoid being trapped by your patience in a superstock that has gone astray? There is no good answer, as the previous illustrations make clear. However, you should be on the alert for sea changes in the company's fortunes, and these can take many forms. One of the most insidious is the company management whose main goal shifts from enhancing shareholder values to self-aggrandizement. Watch out for management perks that reach a grandiose scale. Fleets of corporate aircraft and limousines are a tip-off. When corporate headquarters compete with the Taj Mahal, be on the alert. When Sears built its arrogant tower in downtown Chicago, that was fair warning to stockholders in the company that something was amiss. This is not to imply that corporate headquarters should be anything but a best foot forward. However, when buildings become monuments, look out. Change is in the wind and it's not for the better.

Some companies grow bolder as they grow older. Some managements try to match previous growth rates by taking ever-larger chances. Excessive borrowing leads to uncontrollable leverage that may temporarily inflate earnings but which eventually will become burdensome. The recent leveraged-buyout fiasco financed with junk bonds more than illustrates the point.

Another good barometer to watch is the company's spending on research and development, not in absolute amounts but relative to sales. When this percentage begins to slip, be careful. Above all, keep an eye on the competition, particularly competition's ability to generate new products to increase its share of market.

Too many shareholders fail to read their annual reports and proxy statements. Unfortunately for them, this is where the treasure is buried. Be sure to check the footnotes to the financial material. Some savvy investors begin their reading of the annual reports there. The proxy is often filled with arcane legal language, but the disclosures are meant to inform, not confuse, stockholders.

Lesson

One of the toughest questions an equity investor will face is "When is a lackluster or underperforming stock a real loser and when is it instead simply underappreciated or misunderstood?" The two possibilities are poles apart yet not easily distinguished.

"Well, there's some truth in what we're telling stockholders."

55

Fine Distinctions

Where there's factory smoke, there may be more than profits being generated. In the overzealous pursuit of near-term returns, some managements develop a cavalier attitude toward longer-term risks.

Then they compound the exposure with clever smoke screens of their own.

Strict accounting standards, rigorously applied, help protect shareowners, but the fine-print explanations in company communications are rarely read. Even less noted are the more detailed documents, such as the publicly available 10K and 10Q forms that companies are required to file on a timely basis with the Securities and Exchange Commission. Nevertheless, a careful reading of a company's annual report is a good starting point.

Management, trying aggressively to ramp up earnings, will often turn to the leverage of added indebtedness, but there are practical limits to that tactic. So they resort to additional debt financing, which can be excluded from the company's own balance sheet. Search for these references. The risks are ignored at your peril.

Sometimes apparent growth in a company's earnings stream can be traced to an aggressive acquisition program. If the companies acquired are cheap enough and seem to enjoy relatively superior returns, the appearance of earnings growth will be created. But there are too many opportunities for creative accounting in mergers and acquisitions, and, too often, earnings expectations prove too high or some serious liabilities materialize. Divestiture at a substantial loss illuminates the unseen burden too late, so be on your guard.

Nonoperating revenues are another common smoke screen. Suppose that a company has completed a large financing recently. The proceeds are immediately invested at a high rate of interest. The income flows straight to the bottom line. That looks good at first, but as the money is invested in the business, this income stream dries up, at least temporarily. Unless management has been forthright in its disclosures, that may come as a shock to less perceptive investors. Nonrecurring items also deserve scrutiny. While they usually get separate treatment in financial reports, their role is often overlooked in the emphasis on net profits.

Another familiar corporate smoke screen is the underfunding of pension liabilities. A company may deliberately fail to set aside sufficient funds or otherwise provide for the retirement of its employees. Or it may be substantially underestimating the continually rising costs of health benefits promised retirees. Either failure falsely inflates current earnings, so check the fine print.

Other forms of management inaction can create smoke screens. In an age of rapid technological change, some assets will become obsolete well before their normal depreciation cycle. Responsible managements will write off the difference and take the charge against current earnings. If you don't see such action being taken, you can be sure that current earnings are improperly inflated.

Hidden liabilities have a nasty way of surfacing at the worst possible moment. Avoid the risk by becoming allergic to management smoke screens.

Lesson
In far too many instances, serious risks are buried in the fine print of the annual report. Train yourself to be a careful reader. Let other investors "judge the book by its cover."

"The Bix Corp. merger's off. Go short!"

<u>56</u>

Take the Money and Run

It makes your day when one of your portfolio companies becomes the target of a merger or acquisition offer at well above its current market price. Such good fortune may induce natural giddiness at a time when clear thinking may be required. Since most mergers and acquisitions are fabricated on a solid economic foundation, you will usually have sufficient time for analysis.

Economically speaking, mergers or acquisitions can be separated into two types. In some cases, the surviving company represents no significant improvement over the component companies. In this sense, 1 plus 1 equals 2. These are the weakest unions. You should be alert for a timely opportunity to sell because you can never be certain that the other company may not have undetected problems. In other cases, the surviving company may be much stronger than the component companies. This union results in a number larger than 2. Consequently, despite a nice jump in the value of your holding, your wisest course may be to stay with the combined entity.

Look for signs of synergy. In marketing, the combined companies may have a much fuller product line that improves competitive position. Perhaps sales forces will be better situated geographically or can give more efficient coverage. Or manufacturing facilities can be combined for economies of scale or distribution. The coalition may bring access to new and enlarged markets, for example, foreign opportunities. Maybe financing will be easier to arrange for the new entity. And so on. There are many possibilities, so search for them. Obviously, the managements will attempt to put the rationale for the combination in the best possible light in order to solicit the approval of their shareowners.

While mergers and acquisitions may start out on solid economic ground, there are plenty of ways for deals to fall apart. Too often, corporate personalities prove to be stronger than economics. Irreconcilable arguments over executive rank have scotched otherwise attractive unions. Sometimes audits discover accounting discrepancies that alter the basis for the combination. And so on.

When deals collapse, your glee will turn to anguish in a hurry because the stock's price will plummet to its former level. Consequently, there's a temptation to sell out quickly. However, it may be too quickly. Frequently enough, the first offer prompts a competitive bid at a higher price. And that may lead to a bidding war in which the offering price escalates. How to resolve the dilemma?

Don't be greedy. Competitive bids happen quickly or not at all. When your stock's price rises to within 10 percent of the offering price, it's time to liquidate your holding. If you have made the decision to sell, waiting for that final increment can be dangerous. Remember, the market offers a slew of opportunities for reinvesting the proceeds, so it's not as if you are losing a final opportunity.

Lesson

If you have been the beneficiary of a merger or acquisition windfall, be neither hasty nor complacent. If the combination does not have strong appeal and the stock's price has risen to within 10 percent of the offering terms, sell.

"Let it snow. We're comfy and cozy by the fire. So let's relax and toss some ideas around like 'uncertain economy,' 'stability of principal,' 'budget deficits,' and 'fluctuating stock market.'"

57

No Sweat

It is easy to advise you to "buy stocks when nobody wants them," but it's impractical to give such advice without cautioning that it is next to impossible to use. When individual stocks or the market itself falls out of favor, there will always be reasons offered sufficient to dissolve your good intent. Never mind that these reasons may later turn out to be totally wrong.

To be a successful investor, you must prepare yourself to be both emotionally and intellectually challenged. One way to handle the problem is to do your intellectual homework, the investment research, well in advance. Then you should be prepared to act if an opportunity is presented. Too many investors don't begin their research until after prices have begun to fall, and when the prices fall still further, they become discouraged and lose interest.

Here's a practical hint that helps build experience but causes no financial pain. Do a dry run. Keep a notebook of the "buy" decisions that you are prepared to make. Record the date, the stock's price, and the level of one of the popular stock market indices. The probabilities are strong that these "buy" decisions will prove to be early and unprofitable, unless you happen to find yourself in the throes of a strong market. In any event, you will gather enough data to calculate the percentage change in the stock's price and the percentage change in the market index so that you can see how the stock is moving relative to the market. With a little work, you will soon make some worthy observations. First, you will note the importance of the general trend of the market. Stocks rarely swim against the current. Second, while there may be moments of excitement, the daily up-and-down swings rarely confer usable intelligence. Third, the trend upward is a time-consuming, plodding affair.

If the market is in a strong decline, your efforts will be even more valuable. First you will discover that the market moves much faster on the downside than on the upside. Second, you will find that individual stocks fall much faster than the market as a whole. Third, you will learn how futile it is to attempt to "buy" your stocks of interest at their lowest price. Nothing in the market prevents bargains from becoming even greater bargains. Fourth, while a rising market will hold your interest, a falling market will chill it. The probabilities are that by the time a true bottom has been reached, you will have lost interest in your paper "buys" and joined other investors in the paralyzing fear of what disaster lies ahead next.

The further you progress in this exercise, the more obvious it will be that the secret of investment success lies in self-discipline.

Lesson
The stock market learning process is neither without pain nor effort. One way to ease the burden is to keep a diary of buy or sell decisions that you might have made on stocks of interest to you. Soon enough you will become convinced that the stock market is not the road to easy riches. Later on, you will see how the "paper mistakes" led to better decisions.

"Harvey is sitting on some inside information, but he doesn't know how to use it."

58

Timid Rabbits

Inside information sounds like a sure route to quick profits, but it isn't. Leaving aside the issue of illegality, inside information is a mixed blessing. Sometimes it is difficult to know if the information is good news or bad news. For instance, suppose that you learn that a company is about to raise its prices significantly. Will that improve profitability or will the jump cause the company to lose market share? Maybe others have already heard and acted on the scoop so that the news is now discounted in the stock's price and its public disclosure will invite profit taking. Some insiders watch for an unusual jump in orders to key suppliers. That might seem to signal a sharp upturn in the business. But suppose that the increased orders are actually a hedge against a strike at a key supplier or simply intended to correct an inventory imbalance. The questions usually remain, "Is the inside information based on fact or credible rumor? Is it part of the story or all of it?" Do your homework and leave inside information to the insiders. Once your analysis is complete act decisively.

Doubt makes cowards of us all. What is to be gained if after careful thought and effort in arriving at a decision, you act too cautiously and establish only a token position for your portfolio? If the analysis is correct, an opportunity has been squandered. If incorrect, the negative effect may have been minimized, but think of all the time that has been wasted. Decide in advance that if your research reaches a positive conclusion, your actions will at least match your strong conviction. You will find it almost axiomatic that great investment decisions require equal amounts of courage. The stock market gives no gifts because there is too much competition for great investment ideas.

Excellent opportunities are frequently missed because it is easy to convince yourself that the piecemeal accumulation of a position is somehow a more prudent course. Actually, your indecision is either the result of a lack of courage or the failure to do sufficient research to buttress your resolve. Most investors who take the toe-in-the-water approach never build the positions that they originally intended. Once a stock begins to move up, few are willing to admit they made a mistake at lower price levels and will correct it by paying up. The consequence is that they never reap the rewards due them for their original perception.

The same hazard holds true for selling as well as it does for buying. If part of a holding has been sold, but the stock dives before the total position has been liquidated, advisors will frequently comment, "At least some selling was done at good prices." That's a cop-out. Being partly right is not sufficient solace for having missed real opportunity. If your reasons for selling part of a holding are solidly based, the odds are they are sufficient to justify selling all of it.

Lesson

Reconcile yourself to the reality that a good decision is very hard to make, whether it's a decision to buy or sell. Since the very best decisions are contrary to the popular perception, they will be difficult by their very nature. If you find your decision to be especially troublesome, you are probably on the right track.

<u>59</u>

Hard Realities

The more experience you have with the stock market, the more
the conclusion will become inescapable that *what* you buy is much
more important than *when* you buy. It is enticing to think of the

profit to be made in buying at the low and selling at the high, but that delusion has all the quality of fool's gold. It is possible to find stock after stock that could have been bought at its 52-week high and with patience and a forbearance of its subsequent volatility grew to be a very rewarding investment.

You are practicing another self-delusion if you buy a stock with the attitude that the performance of a newly purchased stock must please you quickly or shortly be sold. There are simply too many extraneous factors affecting the prices of stocks for that to be realistic. Nor is that the degree of conviction which inspires long-term ownership, where the real money is made in the stock market.

Here's another exercise for you. Buy or borrow from your broker a chart book that covers a wide population of stocks. As you thumb through it, your eyes will quickly spot the stocks with outstanding performance. Don't waste time analyzing what might have been or wondering how high the next leg up will go. Instead, look at the stock's performance prior to the run up. Ask yourself, How long was this stock ignored by investors? How many impatient investors missed a great opportunity that was immediately ahead if only they had had a little more patience?

If you are an experienced investor, the chances are better than even that after you have made a commitment, the stock's price will decline. That situation has the makings of a real paradox. Why would any seasoned investor take action that would be susceptible to immediate loss? Well, long ago you learned the perils of chasing "hot" stocks and the virtue in looking for value that others chose to ignore. Why not wait for the price to stop declining? Primarily, because you can't be sure that lower prices will prevail. If your research has been diligent, it is much more important that you close the loop by acting on your efforts.

Some investors refuse to buy a stock unless it is already moving upward. The reasoning is that if they buy a listless stock, it's equivalent to having their money sterilized and unproductive. When the interest of others in the stock is aroused, they take it as an indication that there is validity to their analysis. In their view, it's better to keep the money earning interest as reserves. The flaw in this technique is that much of the upward movement in a stock that breaks out of the doldrums occurs early on. Miss that and you miss a lot.

Lesson
There is no denying that timing is important, but the right choice is even more so.

"I think I've found the trouble. You've been running this business on idle too long. Put her in high and floor it."

<u>60</u>

Blight Future

It seems trite to observe that capital gains in stocks are achieved by buying any issue that is worth more in the future than its value in the present. Obviousness aside, there is food for thought here.

The prospect for future worth cannot be reasonably assessed without appraising present worth. In one sense, it might be argued that a stock's present worth is determined by its last trade in the marketplace. But it's more complicated than that. Just suppose that the last trade vastly undervalued or overvalued the present worth of the company. Then what?

One of the redeeming features of the stock market is the accessibility of corporate information that allows investors to assay a company's intrinsic value. For publicly traded stocks, corporate history and data are freely available from sources like annual reports, SEC documents, financial service write-ups, and analyst reports. Earnings, assets, and liabilities are fully disclosed. So far, so good. The hitch comes in examining the market's historical reaction to this information. You will find that investors are seldom consistent in their judgments of the present worth of corporate basics, even in short time spans. Consequently, the jumping-off place for assessing future worth is a shaky platform at best.

Although the future is written on the wind, it's easy enough to quantify expectations. For example, imagine that you are told about a stock that is expected to double in three years' time. To achieve that goal, the stock's price gain would have to compound at 26 percent annually. Ask yourself, Does that seem reasonable? Would this be an ordinary or extraordinary performance for a company in this industry? If it is a sharp departure from norm, be suspicious.

There is another check on expectations that is commonly used. If a stock has an anticipated value in the future, then that value can be converted to a projected growth rate and compared with the rate of return of some standard investment yardstick, say the rate of return afforded by a government bond to the same point in the future. For example, say you have found an investment that you confidently expect to grow at a 10 percent annual rate for the next five years. In contrast, you find that a government bond maturing in five years will yield 8 percent. Since the government bond is presumed to be riskless, 2 percent per year is your reward for accepting the risks of equity ownership. The reason for this exercise is to get a better perspective on the risk-reward ratio. You must ask yourself if you are being paid enough for the difference between a riskless and a risky investment.

In actual practice, the stock market is much more shortsighted. Experts have found that the price of a stock is mostly correlated with what has happened to the company during the past six months and what may happen to the company in the next six months.

There is a Wall Street saying that "popularity kills opportunity." Even if you pick a stock that has growing earnings, there is seldom much opportunity for capital gains if the company continues to earn in the future at the same rate that it has in the past because that projection is already reflected, most likely, in the price of the stock. Put another way, superior values are best sought among the companies lacking excessive popularity. Since the past is plain for all to view, you must seek those elements that are not readily apparent. This is where knowledge of a particular company or industry can prove quite valuable.

Lesson
When a stock's price climbs without an increase in the attractiveness of the business fundamentals, don't be blinded by your good fortune. Your risk exposure is increasing with every upward trade.

"Luckily, we have a tremendous flow of ideas going through here."

61

To Sky Blue

Trees and companies do not grow to the sky. For individual stocks there even seems to be an unwritten law that growth cannot escape from the ravages of aging any more than human beings can.

Consider the example of the computer giant, IBM, which grew to dwarf its competition and drove such giants as General Electric and RCA from the industry. With that advantage and impossible as it may seem, IBM misjudged the emergence of the personal computer and suffered a serious erosion of its invincible market position. If that wasn't bad enough, Microsoft built a billion-dollar software business under its very nose—an incredible feat. Remember, when you pay a high price for a company's growth you are assuming that this growth will continue for many years ahead. Buying right does little good if you are not prepared to hold on. Holding on will do you no good, it may even do great harm, if you did not buy right in the first place.

It is important that you develop some sense of where a company of possible interest to you stands in its growth cycle. Size alone is no guarantee of a company's continued profitability or longevity. Think of what has happened to some of the giants that are now missing from industries like computers, airlines, railroads, retail stores, and natural resources. On the other hand, familiar corporate giants like Procter & Gamble, 3M, Campbell Soup, Coca Cola, and Merck persist and prosper.

There are two kinds of stimulus to a company's long-term growth—that from within and that from without. Internal growth is most often the result of a vigorous research and development program that feeds the product and service pipeline. Therefore, in analyzing a company's potential for longevity, it is important to inspect the trend of research and development expenditures over some reasonable time frame, say five years. Many companies feature this information in their annual report. It is not the absolute amount that counts, but rather the R&D expenditures as a percent of revenues. All things being equal, a rising trend should be positive and a declining trend a warning.

Growth from sources outside the company are many and varied, yet no less important than internally generated growth. As a good sign of vitality, look for a positive attitude on the part of the company toward joint ventures, licensing agreements, strategic partnering, joint marketing efforts to penetrate foreign markets, and the like. There is an overwhelming tendency for many of the corporate giants to eschew invention, new products, or unique marketing insights unless they were developed in-house. Take this attitude as a sign of hardening of corporate arteries.

Prefer companies whose growth is projected to follow traditional lines of endeavor. When companies stray far from their field in the search for renewed vigor, look out. The track record of such efforts is not very encouraging.

Lesson

When you find yourself tempted to sell a historically well-run company for seemingly good reasons, do so very carefully. Remind yourself that such companies rarely change their positive characteristics in the short term. Recognize that more likely than not, what concerns you is the price action of the stock, not the integrity of the company.

"The wire services say the market has gone to hell in a handbasket. Shouldn't we be panicking and selling and jumping out of windows?"

62

You First

Following the stock market crowd is a good way to lighten your pocketbook and lose your financial shirt, particularly if your preference is for short-term trading. At no time is this more true than when the market is trading at its extremes. Usually by the time you get the drift of what's going on in the market, professional speculators are switching the direction of their strategies. They always seem to be one step ahead of you, but there is more to their art than just timing.

The art of stock speculation in one sense is built on the ability to recognize when a seeming risk is not a real risk or when a real risk is not nearly as great as it appears to be. To wit, suppose that the stock market has experienced a dramatic decline. Longer-term investors are shaken by the event and become inactive. The professional speculators, on the other hand, know their market history. No market, not even a full-blown bear market, declines in a straight line downward. There will be brief periods when the market comes up for air. At times like these, the risk of decline is more apparent than real and the pros are ready to take advantage. Another illustration. Suppose that a security analyst who's recognized as an expert in an institutional favorite decides to lower the firm's rating from "buy" to "strong hold." The rationalization is that the price of the stock has simply gotten ahead of its story. What often happens? Selling panic develops, but professional investors who can distinguish between seeming risk and real risk find opportunity at the expense of the herd.

If you have the nerve for it, it is easier to do speculative buying in down markets than to engage in speculative short selling in robust up markets. The reason is that "bad" news or surprises tend to bring frantic selling by those anxious to liquidate their portfolio positions. If the stock has been an institutional favorite, the effect will be all the more dramatic. This herd reaction explains why such stocks have been known to drop 20 to 30 percent in price in a single day. It's tempting to react to an opportunity like that, particularly if you think that the company's trouble may be temporary. However, you will find that there will be institutional sellers who are just plain slow to react to the news. Selling pressure might not abate soon and, in fact, will most likely increase for a while. Notwithstanding, bad news that has been overdiscounted in a stock's price does represent real opportunity.

Another serviceable adage on Wall Street goes, "Never short a 'hot' dog." This means that the irrationality that pushes a stock of questionable value to ever-greater heights is most likely to persist well beyond the point where it is obvious to all. This also applies to taking a profit in a strong market. Some of the largest gains in stocks are registered at the very end of a bull move.

Lesson

Successful speculation is more than a willingness to accept well-above-average risk. It's more than a product of sharp timing or the hope for extraordinary good luck. Take a clue from the professional speculators. For them, it is the art of distinguishing between real and apparent risk.

"We share your disappointment over your account performance, so we've come up with some dandy fresh ideas."

<u>63</u>

Unreasonable Reason

When stocks fail to perform up to expectations, there is an almost irresistible urge to sell out and make a fresh start. The recommendation has a special appeal because the "mistakes" of the past are soon forgotten. Moreover, you can also bet that when your advisor or broker offers new recommendations, they will be brimming with opportunity that far overshadows the old. When you think about it, it's much the same idea as celebrating on New Year's Eve by ringing out the inevitable disappointments of the old year and hailing the bright prospects of the new. Experience shows the futility of it all, but that doesn't stop us.

However, in the midst of the hope for the future, there is a sobering thought worth considering. Remember that the stock you are about to purchase as a fresh, new idea is a tired, old idea to the seller. For you to execute a trade, someone must see the end of opportunity or the heightening of risk to an unacceptable level. Then there is the other side: the stock you are selling is, to its buyer, a fresh, new story. The irony should not be wasted.

When stocks lag the performance of their peers, it is natural to be disappointed for two reasons. First, because your hindsight reveals an obvious error in judgment, and second, because you will also be aware of having missed any number of opportunities that would have provided handsome returns. It's that same sinking feeling that comes when you have chosen a horse that is behind the pack and apparently not going to make up lost ground. Time to tear up the ticket and prepare for the next race. But that is exactly where investors go wrong, for their race literally never ends. There is no finish line for the stock market.

First things first. Recognize that it is much easier to clean out an unhappy position than it is to do the kind of research work it would take to make sure that the old position now lacks the opportunity once foreseen. Spend as much time on what you are selling as on what you are buying. Maybe there were reasons for the lackluster performance. Maybe there is a real opportunity at hand to make up for lost ground.

If you are mentally prepared to recognize the bias in "new" recommendations, you will be in a better position to make a sound judgment. Occasionally, your advisors will adapt a variation on the "out with the old" theme. They will present a "new" recommendation and suggest that in the search for funds to execute it they have found a "tired" stock that has failed to live up to expectations. Not so fast.

Lesson

Don't let disappointment with a stock's performance overshadow your judgment. When you are thinking of substituting one stock for another, don't be casual in reviewing the stock earmarked for sale. Usually it is the worst performer in the portfolio that gets the axe without regard to the company's favorable attributes.

"The market is plunging! The market is plunging!"

64

Psyched Down

It may sound like heresy, but stock performance has become more closely allied with shifts in investor psychology and less closely tied to prospective changes in the business outlook. In fact, many of the dramatic changes in investor attitudes have been occurring without any significant change in earnings anticipations. Unhappily, the perfection of worldwide communications has brought a seemingly boundless supply of assaults, alarms, and excursions to shatter investor tranquility. Changes in currency exchange rates induce huge pools of liquid assets to move rapidly in and out of domestic stock markets. And that's not all.

Listen to the business news reports, and you will frequently hear how computer-based buying or selling activity brought about an abrupt change in the market's direction. While that might seem to be a new market force at work, it's really more of the same. Computer trading models are designed to detect subtle differences between investor expectations as expressed in the index options market and the underlying value of the index stocks based on current trading. You are entitled to your opinion as to the worth of these gymnastics, but the fact is they are here to stay for the foreseeable future. It helps to recognize that the fault lies not with modeling techniques, but with the fact that too many large investors are trying to do the same thing at the same time.

The wonder of it is that the market has maintained any composure at all. That's not a grumble, but a serious observation. All things considered, the market in the broad perspective has responded relatively well. The reason is only conjecture, but it may not be too wide of the mark. An old, but tested, market adage has it that the market never discounts the same thing twice. Most of the forces that are impinging on market psychology are old news. However, the fallout from all of this is bound to be the increased volatility of stock prices. No investor likes to see the prices of portfolio flit aimlessly about, but the only antidote seems to be increased forbearance.

Perhaps one effect of the volatility resulting from the ascending role of market psychology over earnings trends will be more emphasis on the creation of long-range values and less emphasis on short-term swings. Another effect may be a general lowering of price-to-earnings ratios because investors will want some compensation for enduring erratic prices. Whatever the practical effect, it will pay to keep an eye on the big picture and watch for indications of how well the stock market handles its broader influences. There should be signs to guide you. When earnings disappointments cause precipitous drops in individual stocks, take that as a sign that investor psychology is souring. When the same disappointments have little negative effect, read that as a positive sign. The market's traditional psychological guideposts have been fear and greed, but new influences are increasing in importance.

Lesson
Market averages record the market's movements, but wise investors watch for change in its inner dynamics as well.

"Goodbye, dear. Have a good day and don't forget to step back once in awhile and look at the larger picture."

65
Crystal-Balling It

When you attempt to outguess the stock market, be humble. You're pitting your personal judgment against the distilled wisdom of some of the best brains in the world. But neither be dismayed. Nobody, professional or neophyte, knows for certain what the future will hold, and the future is what it's all about. Moreover, even among investment professionals, there are those who insist on earning their skills the hard way—through bitter experience with poor decisions. Nevertheless, all must make some rational judgments about the larger prospects and, hopefully, educated guesses will turn out better than wild ones. Investors should bear in mind that market excesses stem mostly from the inability to foresee the future rather than from investor or managerial stupidity.

The challenge for investors is compounded because company managements too are subject to the limitations imposed by the necessity of divining the future. Not only must they make judgments about their own businesses and their competitors' activities, but they must make decisions based on their anticipation of changes in the big picture, that is, the national and international economy. Boiled down, this means that investors must make guesses about guesses.

Small wonder there is so much inconsistency of investment performance among experienced professionals. Today's so-called all-stars have the unfortunate habit of fading all too quickly from the limelight. Yet the media continue to report investment performance weekly as if it were just another ball score. The rotation of the players should be tip-off enough that the exercise is flaky.

Why do professional investors so enthusiastically absorb the daily flow of economic reports? It's because today is the jumping-off place for the future. How can you project the future if you are unsure of where you are now? The trouble is that investors and economists use this information to make projections. Most often, they will look for trends in the big picture. Other times they look for similarities with past events or developments. The flaw is that though the patterns may appear the same, very different forces can be at work so that the appearance is only accidental and the trap for the unwary has been set.

If you feel overwhelmed, take heart. A good dose of humility is a perfect antidote for unrealistic expectations. While the distant future is mostly obscured, events in the immediate future as a rule resemble those of the immediate past. The economic and business forces that matter most to long-term investors are so large and powerful that they rarely switch direction in an instant. Forecast you must; just don't forget the underlying frailty of the system.

Lesson

The stock market causes much distraction. It's up to you to get its drift by keeping an eye on the future.

"The fireworks tonight will be provided by Mr. Wilson N. Conroy after he learns his company lost $1.2 million in the last quarter."

66

On Display

Shortfalls in expected company earnings are an ugly sight. Usually they are accompanied by sharp price declines and heavy turnover. Knowing what to do about them is the problem. Often you will find that these stocks have been weak for several days prior to the disappointing announcement. By the time that you get the information you need in order to make a judgment, that information is too late to be effective.

Given all the variables and unknowns that must be accounted for in an earnings projection, it's hard to understand why the shortfalls have such a profound effect on market prices. Those in the best position to make estimates, the company's senior management, are the least inclined to make their internal projections public. Not only do they recognize the tenuousness of such efforts, they don't want to be accused of misleading their stockholders. However, investment analysts fearlessly fill the breach. With their financial models of the company, they figure out future earnings to a fraction of a cent. That's good mental discipline, but these best guesses are too often confused with whole truth. When the projections fail to match up with reality, the analysts are the first ones to cry "foul."

Actually, the analysts occupy a privileged position. Many of them have followed their specialty companies for several years. Consequently, they can pick up on the nuances in their conversations with management. Furthermore, while managements are wise not to give earnings estimates or to comment on analysts' projections, they will offer "guidance." When bad news is imminent, analysts are sometimes given a not-so-veiled warning. The thought is to let the stock down easy. The trouble comes when the analysts pass these misgivings on to their firms' institutional clients before the company makes the disclosure. Lately, some managements have made prompt announcements of shortfalls in their anticipated earnings a month or more before they are formally released. In that way the effect is much better diffused. When a company delays its earnings announcements, that's another warning. Chances are better than even that, when released, the news will be poor. The delay most likely is caused by management's harried efforts to put a better face on the news.

The more experience you gain from watching the reaction to earnings shortfalls, the more confused you may become. For instance, there will be occasions when a stock will rise on the announcement. That is because the news is already reflected in the price of the stock and the announcement is anticlimactic. You will also note that the severity of the reaction depends upon whether the stock had a high price-to-earnings ratio or whether it had been a market favorite of late. Finally, there is no ignoring the importance of the general trend of the market. If the market is in a strong uptrend, the earnings disappointment will frequently be shrugged off. Conversely, when the market is in a sharp downtrend, expect the negative effect to be exaggerated.

Lesson
A "poor" earnings announcement might be expected to lead to declining prices for a stock, but it doesn't always happen that way. Sometimes stocks will seemingly defy logic by rising. The variety of market responses to "poor" earnings news illustrates the complexity of the stock market game.

"Then I told the trustees that if 'trained seals' could outperform us, they must be better paid."

67

Pay Up

Investment advice may or may not be worth the expense. It depends on whether or not the recommendations given help you achieve your investment goals. In a pragmatic sense that means making profits and avoiding losses. But suppose that you were told that you only had to pay for gains and would be charged nothing for advice that led to losses. If that sounds appealing, think it through.

In the very nature of the stock market, losses are inevitable. Since all investment guidance is based on incomplete information and guessing the unknowable, advice that was sound when given often enough turns sour. Losses are not a sufficient excuse for avoiding payment for services rendered. Yet there is a healthy, ingrained desire in all of us to get our money's worth. So how to judge? The process is not only difficult, it's full of traps.

Take a simple example. Assume that the advice rendered to you was restricted to only buy or sell recommendations on individual stocks. Offset the winners against the losers, and you have an exact answer to the "money's worth" question. Or do you? Even if the results are positive, can you be sure that they are directly traceable to the advice given? Suppose that your profit came mostly from a strong market rally and was not due to any change in the fortunes of the companies held in your portfolio. Or suppose that the advice was profitable, but for the wrong reasons. What is this advice worth?

If you think it through, you'll see that a lot of subjective judgment goes into the process of determining whether investment advice is worth its cost. Consequently, it's easy to get so bound up with the exercise that it becomes counterproductive.

In your appraisal, stick to the basics. Free advice is worth what you pay for it. This especially applies to stock tips from friends and acquaintances. Some of the old-line investment advisory services are true bargains at their price. They collect enormous amounts of pertinent data and format it in ways that are extremely useful to investors. However, treat a service's recommendations for action with a little disrespect, since as a rule they tend to follow rather than lead. If you choose not to be a subscriber, at least ask your broker for tear sheets from the service on stocks of interest to you.

Your broker's commissions are partly payment for the mechanics of the business and partly payment for advice. Good brokers will always put the long-term interests of their clients ahead of a marginal transaction. Nevertheless, taking a larger-than-normal commission, say on an underwriting or a secondary distribution, is a strong temptation for a broker. Don't be bashful. Ask your broker for the percentage of the offering price represented by the gross commission. Be very cautious when the percentage is well above normal.

When you pay for investment advice, take it as given. Second guessing adds nothing but your biases to the process. Be prepared to be patient and realistic in your expectations. If you have misgivings, be forthright about them. You will find that your advisor is well prepared to defend the recommendations rendered.

Lesson
Badly formulated advice is much too expensive, even if free. On the other hand, sound counsel that generates competitive returns is always bargain-priced.

"Yes, Ms. Brimley, we truly respect your woman's intuition, but the firm's hunch is to bet a bunch."

68

Fickle Forebodings

Make no mistake. Managing your equity investments is a demanding, unrelenting, and unforgiving exercise. Professionals learn that lesson early on. Take your eye off the road, and you may be in for trouble. It's what lies ahead that counts; history is already reflected in today's prices.

However, the would-be forecaster is bedeviled by two problems. The first is accumulating all the relevant information that might have an effect on valuations. That turns out to be a flat-out impossibility; there's too much to cover. Even when you've reduced it to what you think is most essential, there's yet another obstacle. To handle voluminous amounts of information, much of it must be put in numeric form. And, most often, that leads to totaling the raw data and creating averages.

Unlike baseball batting averages, financial averages may poorly reflect the meaning of the supporting data. The reason is that averages are weakest when they cover a wide range of data, which is the usual case with data pertinent to investing. What this means is that investment forecasts are launched from very unsteady platforms.

The second problem will be recognized instantly as the worse of the two. The future is not only unknown, but in some instances unknowable. If seeing the past clearly is a near-impossibility, anticipating the future is a real backbreaker. No wonder the forecasters, whether for the economy, the market, or individual investments, fudge a bit.

But note something curious. Pronouncements by investment experts always have the ring of personal authority. While they may hem and haw a bit, the experts eventually say something definite. Those who endlessly straddle the options will soon be seeking employment in some other line of work. Also note that when experts blunder, they're right back with their next forecast, unabashed.

This has all the makings of a paradox. The input side is best guesses, estimates, and hunches. The output side is judgments, forecasts, and predictions delivered with conviction.

It takes the ensuing hard realities to ultimately dissolve the paradox. Although uncertainty is the investor's lot, that does not mean that uncertainty should be met with indecision and wavering. Sophisticated investors learn early on that decisions must be firm and prompt. Vacillation can be deadly. So to cope, they discipline themselves to literally bet a bunch on an educated hunch.

And there's more. While decisions must be made with conviction, they should be reversible with equal conviction. There is no room for emotional entanglements. Managing investments should always be an intellectual activity. Love-hate relationships with individual investments are an invitation to mistakes.

Lesson

Don't be fooled by the predictions of experts. There are more than enough ways for them to be wrong. The more famous the forecaster, the less likelihood that error will be confessed early enough to help. Keep your eye on the future. Trust your commonsense judgments to serve you well, and be prepared to act upon them.

"The latest report has the rising indicators falling and the falling indicators rising."

69

Misleading Indicators

Who's right? For that judgment you have to turn from the headlines to the finer print. But chances are you won't find the answer there either. The media have little appetite for long or complicated explanations of economic or financial matters.

Keep it short and simple is the rule. That's O.K. for superficial news, but investors need more. They need to know how expert opinions have been derived. Sure, it doesn't hurt if some authority is right for the wrong reason, but how long can you count on that kind of luck?

You probably noticed that the media have a penchant for quoting expert viewpoints that oppose one another. Perhaps they only want to appear unbiased. Or it may be simply a desire to serve up something for everyone's plate. Hardly a revelation, but media impartiality causes problems for investors.

First, opposing expert opinions create uncertainty. Almost immediately, the thought that they both might be wrong is eliminated on the assumption that one expert must be right. But which one? Usually the truth lies in between, but the damage is done if an investor is psychologically immobilized and unable to react properly.

Another problem with experts is that they come to believe their own press notices. As they rise in pundit status, they paint themselves further and further into corners. After all, what are experts for if they can't speak with complete authority? The fact that these renowned authorities rise and fall with regularity doesn't act as a deterrence. What is center stage for, except to entertain, particularly when the audience cries for more? Growing media exposure seems to move the experts' public pronouncements further out on the extreme, where they are bound to be newsworthy. Eventually, the experts fall victim to their own excesses, but that's not much comfort to the misled.

Media professionals sometimes fit the biases of experts to the news. They know whom to call. If a financial news development is bearish, they'll call an expert who is known to be bearish. That has the makings of a trap. When investors are nearing emotional extremes in their attitudes, note that expert quotes will be in line with the trend. Experts who have been correct in their predictions will find the opportunity to say, "I told you so," irresistible. And those who were wrong become allergic to media coverage. It's important to recognize the phenomena. Being a contrary investor at market extremes is difficult enough, but biased media coverage makes it more so.

Another problem is the thirst for instant reactions to some major economic or financial news event. It would take an unusually courageous pundit to respond honestly with "I don't know" or "I need more time to think about it." Even worse, much relevant economic news is revised at a later date, but the revision receives meager attention.

Beware of authorities who speak with conviction void of any pertinent qualifiers. It makes for good media coverage, but for the investor, it's probably more distracting than enlightening.

Lesson
Remember that divergent opinions between recognized authorities make for good copy and reader interest. However, for the investor, they may act to compound an already confusing situation.

"Please don't take this too negatively, but they are no longer quoting your stock."

70

Learning Curve

Nothing in the economic world has worth unless somebody else wants it. No matter how rare, precious, or costly to manufacture, anything is worth what someone else will pay for it and not a dime more. Said another way, your investments will be better managed if you develop a healthy respect for the judgment of the market-place. It is pointless to rail against the sellers when a stock you own dives deep into loss territory. The work of all investors is to anticipate the future, and your opposites may have done a more thorough job of foreseeing change in worth than you have.

Most investors thoroughly prepare themselves for good news, but very few care to anticipate bad news with the same diligence. However, it is exactly by thinking about those miserable risks that are bound to surface from time to time that investors can steel themselves against overemotional and counterproductive reactions.

When you are advised to take a chance, step back from the gambling table; the stock market is not Las Vegas. If you can con-trol your appetite for risk, the market presents many opportunities for reasonable speculation. But begin by facing reality. "Sure thing" and "speculation" are terms that should never be used in the same breath. Above all, don't let the dream of exceptional opportunity overwhelm the need to recognize risks.

If you find yourself addressing a speculation whose payoff is based on the assumption that certain high risks will not material-ize, exercise great caution. As a rule, avoid these dice rolls. However, successful speculations are often based on fragmentary information or the immediately unknowable. For instance, sup-pose that a company's financial future could be greatly enhanced by the award of a very large contract, as frequently happens in the defense industry. These facts may be well known, but the impact of the contract is not reflected in the current price of the stock. That's opportunity. However, if you have reason to believe that the company has a decided competitive edge, now you have a rea-sonable speculation.

Heaven forbid that a newcomer's first speculation is a big hit. Mild speculative interest can turn quickly into an addiction.

Worse still is when speculation turns to entertainment. But, you say, it's the other fellow who's in it for the entertainment. Here's a little test. You buy a stock. What originally attracted you to the company was a highly profitable new product that will be introduced within six months. You're satisfied that this development is not widely known. At the current price, you should be able to reap a handsome profit in the stock. Your broker executes your order and reports back to you. What happens? An hour later, you call back and ask, "How's it doing?" That's entertainment! Experienced investors are much more disciplined.

Lesson

There is a big difference between reckless chance taking and accepting reasonable speculative risk. Be especially wary of trading on tips and rumors, as experience will demonstrate that these rarely pan out.

"Dear Mrs. Throgbottom: As much as it would give our firm pleasure, we cannot in good conscience promise to sell all your stocks before the next crash."

71

Promise
Her Anything?

Some markets give clear evidence of overheating and then fall. Some markets present no evidence of overstimulation and fall anyway. The converse is also true. So, if someone promises you a forewarning of a major market move, you should be leery at best. Recognize that surprises are a hallmark of the stock market. However, if major market trends are not highly predictable, the reaction of the media to them is.

When the stock market has experienced a dramatic move, either up or down, watch out for the "I told you so" crowing of the experts. The media are only too happy to provide such experts a high profile because investment success is worthy news and media readers and viewers appreciate their heroes. Unfortunately, in the media's haste to report the topical, important details are most often lost along the way. For instance, interviews with the newly crowned "experts" rarely reveal how long their views have been held. Would you believe, sometimes for years? Somehow or other, the "stopped clock" types are rarely exposed for the interval when they have been false prophets. If you hear of an investor who has rightly divined a recent major market move, but whose timing was way off, probabilities are that this "hero" is a net loser.

Rarer still are the interviews that get into the rationalizations behind the "expert's" opinion. Suppose that a market expert is right for the wrong reasons. It happens, but the revelation would take some serious probing. What expert would want to confess error at the height of media exposure? Besides, extensive rationalizations do not qualify as being newsworthy.

When you judge the business news, there is something else to keep in mind. While interviewers try to be accurate in their reporting of expert opinions, they are nonetheless influenced by current trends. Thus, if bearish attitudes prevail and the economic prognosis is poor, there is a noticeable tendency on the part of media personnel to seek out experts who have a consistent bearish bias to their opinions. Likewise on the bull side. If this coloration prevails long enough, it contributes to an overbought and oversold market.

Consequently, you may find yourself being swayed by reported expert opinion that is subtly and unduly one-sided. If that continues long enough, it may be hard to buck the trend at precisely the time you should do so. When the bullish or bearish opinions of the experts become too consistent, it is time to assume that the stock market is overdiscounting the reported news.

Lesson

Listening to the experts explaining their most recent successful stock market or economic predictions is not only a waste of time, it's another example of following the news. Too much time spent in this pursuit becomes habit-forming and distracts you from your goal of anticipating the news.

"In an effort to increase productivity, we're going to restructure middle management into three groups—the ants, the bees, and the beavers."

<u>72</u>

Ungraceful Aging

One of the biggest challenges facing an investor who insists on owning the "blue chips" is identifying those companies that are losing the very vitality that made them great. Since the geriatric process takes place gradually, it is not easily detectable. In fact, managements go to considerable lengths to disguise or hide this condition. As an example, take mighty General Motors, the world's largest automobile manufacturer and dominant factor in its industry. Once thought to be invincible, GM is now thought to be an also-ran.

It is a common investment mistake to confuse size with vitality. Remember that by the time successful companies approach their maturity, they most likely have accumulated more than their fair share of unproductive assets and personnel. It might be argued that the present trend among the "blue chips" toward "downsizing" and "restructuring" is evidence of continued vitality. That claim would be more believable if the managements now overseeing the process weren't the very same ones who created the so-called excesses in the first place. The risk is that the cure may turn out to be worse than the disease.

The annual report is a good place to look for hardening of business arteries. Beware of managements who sound on the defensive and heartily embrace retrenchment rather than preparing for the opportunities that lie ahead. Whenever you detect an overemphasis on the company's traditions or precedents, look out. Also watch out for those corporate egomaniacs who think mostly about making their company bigger when they should be concerned with making it more profitable.

Another danger sign to watch for is competitors who are successfully poaching on what was once considered the company's private preserve. Well-run companies keep close tabs on their competitors and use every legitimate means to insulate their competitive advantage from erosion. If you begin to see superior appeal in a competitor's new offerings, be on the alert. In an era of rapid technological change, there's a hazard that obsolescence has not been properly reflected in the plant and equipment account. A company may be correctly depreciating its assets, but that's small comfort if the company is delaying a major modernization program in order to buttress current earnings. Write-offs due to plant closings and consolidations have become fairly common and should be taken as a sign of the tardy recognition of competitive realities.

Still another poor omen is the buy-back of company stock in the open market. This may be a legitimate use of corporate reserves in that shares outstanding are reduced and earnings-per-share reports are enhanced. Even so, what these companies are really saying is that they can't find growth opportunities in other or allied business areas that offer returns on investment equal to or greater than their present returns on invested capital. That's a sad commentary on their vision—and an indication of corporate glaucoma.

Lesson
Recognize that some blue-chip companies age gracefully, while others do not. To ignore the latter is to endanger your investment health.

"All those in favor of staying afloat by dipping into the sinking fund, say 'Aye.'"

73

A Borrower Be?

Should you own stocks on margin? That depends. Too many investors have had sad experiences with margin borrowing. At the other extreme are those who never have borrowed and never intend to borrow to enlarge their equity exposure. Somewhere in between are the fortunate few wise enough to know when to borrow and how much.

In simplest terms, the cost of margin borrowing is the price of time. What really matters is whether the time being bought is used profitably or not. Suppose that your account is fully invested when the stock market goes into an unexpected tailspin, and the shock, plus the effect of margin calls, panics investors. Surely conditions such as these would frighten even sophisticated investors, thus creating true bargains. It is tough enough under these conditions to take action, but it's even tougher if you have to do it with margin borrowing. However, these conditions may represent real opportunity instead of apparent risk. If convinced, take the plunge.

How much should you borrow? Part of the answer depends on your tolerance of risk and your stomach for market volatility. The rest of the answer depends upon your personal goals. Before you find yourself too bound up in the odds of winning and losing and how much, concentrate on what you expect from your equity investments and why. That may sound complicated, but for the investor there are only two goals.

First, you may aim to maintain your financial position relative to society as a whole. This implies that you have amassed sufficient wealth to satisfy your wants, but you want to use equity positions to offset the long-term ravages of inflation. Under this scenario, margin borrowing seems ill-advised. Second, you may be striving to improve your relative financial position. For instance, you recognize that retirement will mean a substantial reduction in your standard of living. Your investment goal is to build assets and fill the gap. Unfortunately, the long-term returns from the stock market imply that you will be unable to reach your objective. Under that scenario, the use of margin borrowing to buy quality issues at bargain prices is an alternative for you that deserves serious consideration.

If you are one of those unfortunates who experienced a margin call in a plunging market, you probably have been scarred for life. Chances are that you were holding on to your positions with the self-delusion that the market couldn't possibly go much lower. But it did. And when it did, you found yourself forced to liquidate positions that looked cheaper than ever imaginable. The experience was a nightmare. The probabilities are that you did your borrowing when the market was rising and late in its cycle. It's a mistake to swear off margin borrowing because of that one sad experience. Next time use your leverage for true bargain hunting.

Lesson

Using other people's money, i.e., your broker's, to enlarge your equity portfolio is not necessarily good or bad. It may be either, depending on circumstances and your temperament. Paradoxically, margin borrowing is best used by the faint-hearted, not the fearless.

"I just want to make it clear before we start that the cards spot trends but don't give specific stock recommendations."

74

It's a Deal

Who wouldn't love to find a superperformance stock? But where do you start to look? Why not start with today's superwinners? If anything is clear from stock market history, it's that powerful trends have a tendency to persist. It takes a long time for great inventions and ideas to reach maturity, and some, after decades of existence, are still on the growth track.

The genesis of these winning investments is found in radical changes. Superficial departures from the norm may represent truly creditable progress, but they are not the stuff that most superwinners are made of. Here are some thoughts to aid your quest.

Search for inventions that satisfy a long-standing want. A few obvious examples from the past are such fundamental breakthroughs as the automobile, which brought mobility and facilitated the transportation of goods; the airplane, which shrunk travel time over great distances; antibiotics, which fought uncontrolled bacterial infections; and the radio, which made possible wireless communications anywhere. And don't stop your search at the main breakthroughs. Think, for instance, of the hundreds of very successful businesses that followed in the wake of emerging computer technology.

Then look for new methods or equipment that can sharply increase productivity, such as fully automated production lines. Next, search for labor-saving devices that improve quality while lowering costs—such as the now-ubiquitous copying machine and robotic production facilities. Also be on the lookout for new and cheaper sources of energy, such as photovoltaics. Seek out ways of avoiding ecological damage, as through recycling or substitution of bioerodible materials.

Science, technology, communications, new materials, computers, greater knowledge—all are the agents of change. To illustrate, consider how much the common, ordinary telephone has changed over the past several years. No longer is the telephone chained to its transmission lines. Telephones are now portable or cellular. No longer are the signals mainly voice transmission. Analog sound has been joined by the digital transmission of massive amounts of data. And those copper transmission wires have been replaced with fiber-optic wires or electronic signals broadcast into space to satellites that bounce the signals back to earth stations. These changes have been so gradual that the investment opportunity in them is frequently overlooked. Additionally, such sweeping changes open up new business opportunities such as bank by phone, catalog shopping, and electronic mail.

Force yourself to think of where today's trends are leading. The advances on medical frontiers due to biotechnology will ultimately satisfy many long-standing human wants. That means that people can be expected to lead longer, more productive lives. What business opportunities will be created and which of today's companies can be expected to be beneficiaries of such powerful trends? Smart investors should be alert for what other investors are overlooking. Wall Street does not have a corner on imagination. Find a new product or service that flows from great change and look into it.

Lesson
Superwinning stocks start their run from great change. You don't have to be early on board, just spot the correct trend in time.

"*Welcome! The box lunch today includes caviar, pheasant and truffles, baked Alaska, and champagne—all little clues to the bottom line of the treasurer's report.*"

75

Winning Recipe

An unexpected earnings breakout is almost guaranteed to brighten a stockholder's day, even without the embellishments. The question is, How do you spot them early enough to make an enviable profit? The answers are many, but here are some of the common ones:

- Look for companies that have fallen from favor but where there is solid evidence of strenuous efforts to turn the company's fortunes around. Keep in mind, however, there is a peculiar characteristic to the way these stocks act. The danger in turnaround situations is that other potential investors will ignore the company's recovery until it is far along. That means that, if early, your investment will flounder until the announcement of an earnings breakout so large that the company's new virtues can no longer be ignored. The ensuing price leap may more than justify your too-early patience.

- Watch for changes in the supply-and-demand relationships for basic commodities. When supply contracts dramatically or demand expands unexpectedly, the leverage produced by even small increases in prices can have a dramatic effect on the earnings of companies in related industries. Remember what happened to oil company earnings when Middle East supplies were curtailed. Weather-based surprises are another source of such opportunities. However, you must be prepared to act quickly because the opportunity is so obvious.

- Keep an eye on companies introducing major new products or entering broad new markets. These activities most often are a serious drag on earnings in their early stages, but once they gather momentum, the effect on earnings can be very substantial.

- Be alert to major changes in a company's capital structure. When an all-equity company sees extraordinary opportunity far beyond its present capital resources, it may borrow heavily. That should serve as your cue to keep a closer eye on the company's activities. Since it takes time for the borrowings to produce the effect intended, you should watch for a jump in the revenue stream first. Since there are always start-up costs and heavy marketing expenses, the impact on earnings usually comes with a lag.

- Seek out companies that are intelligently restructuring their businesses so as to increase the rate of return on their invested capital or to enhance the focus and effectiveness of marketing efforts. Heavy write-offs are a painful distraction, but when properly executed they can be the prelude to sharp gains in earnings.

- Recognize that shifts in currency exchange rates can be another source of unexpected earnings breakouts. Perhaps the best that can be said about the rates is that they fluctuate. The financial media report constantly on the status of the U.S. dollar. What you need to do is watch for companies whose earnings are severely penalized when the dollar is weak relative to other world currencies. Then when the dollar is strong you will know where to look for the opposite effect.

The secret to anticipating earnings breakouts lies in knowing where to look. In this regard, experience will be a great teacher.

Lesson
Earnings breakouts are a thrill, but finding them is a drill.

Stock Evaluation
Checkoff List

To Err Is Human, But...
Safety First for Shareowners

Imagine your discomfort. At takeoff, you learn that your pilot has ignored the preflight checkoff exercise because it is "old familiar stuff." Yet how many stock investors have that same cavalier attitude toward safety checks on their current holdings or possible portfolio additions? The result? Equity positions are exposed to avoidable mistakes. Picks are far chancier than necessary, and are sometimes disastrous.

Think about it. Shareowners confront more oversight risks than the pilot executing preflight drill. But given the host of things that drive stocks up and down, small wonder they're put off by the chore. Fortunately, the burden is manageable if a goal is kept firmly in mind.

What investors need most is a recognition of what *must* go right for equity investments to succeed and where things are *likely* to go wrong. A checkoff list streamlines that search into a logical, step-by-step process. By highlighting the essentials, it yields tightly focused, decision-oriented information. Sure it's work, but eliminating costly oversights is well worth the effort.

The beginning is easy enough. It's simply a company profile drawn with enough detail to provide a basic perspective. The information can be obtained from a stockbroker or from readily accessible financial resources. A sample profile appears on the next page.

Description

Company _____ (   ) Industry Group _____
                  (Symbol)

Shares Outstand._____ mil. Price _____ Market Value $ _____ mil.
        (Fully diluted)

Earnings $_____ P-E _____ Long-Term Debt _____% Equity _____%
     (12 mos. trailing per share)   (Percent of total capitalization)

Dividend $_____   Yield _____%   5-Year Govt. Bond Yield _____%
    (Per share)

Many investors unwittingly bypass this preliminary step, unaware that what appears as commonplace information offers a wealth of insights. For example, look what can be gained from filling in the blanks of the sample profile given above.

- **Industry Group** _____
  How the market and the economy have treated a company's peer group in the past opens a window on the future. Some industry groups are notorious for their sensitivity to the economic cycle. Others are infamous for their wide price swings relative to the market. And so on. It's vain in most instances to argue that a company is "different" and therefore insulated from moves by its industry group.

- **Shares Outstanding** _____ mil. (fully diluted)
  If abnormally large numbers of shares are outstanding, it will take major developments to impact either per share earnings or their multiplier. But if the number outstanding appears reasonable, be sure that it won't be enlarged substantially by subsequent conversions of senior securities into equity.

- **Market Value $** _____ mil.
  Few investors consider the importance of market value, i.e., current price times shares outstanding. However, it is market value that determines whether a company will be large enough to attract the attention of institutional analysts or be so small that it will require constant advocacy from much less powerful

sources. Remember that the stocks of large market value companies perform differently than the stocks of small ones, and that difference needs to be taken into account.

- **Earnings $**_____ **P-E** _____ (12 mos. trailing per share)
Company earnings are best studied as a trend, but the ratio of price over earnings (P-E) is the shortcut to the market's present judgment about the company's future. When the price represents a high multiple of earnings for the preceding 12 months, substantial, positive developments are being anticipated. They must occur for the investment to succeed. When the multiple is rather low, be alert for signs of trouble or advancing maturity.

- **Long-Term Debt** _____% **Equity** _____% (percent of total capitalization)
The company's balance sheet reveals how much debt is used to leverage the company's earning power. Historically, a high proportion of debt relative to total capitalization is a danger sign. That's particularly true if the company's business is sensitive to broad economic cycles. Occasionally, high debt may be characteristic of the company's industry, and therefore the company's debt lies within tolerable limits.

These questions go to the very heart and soul of successful investing. To illustrate their scope and importance consider the following elaboration.

- *Are there special aspects to the business that justify investor interest?* Is the company a major and timely beneficiary of some powerful social, scientific, economic, or business trend? Is there a large untapped demand for its products or services? Is the company a true leader or innovator? Does it possess singular attributes such as market dominance, strong patent position, unique distribution facilities, solid customer franchises? Coming up with the right answers will move the odds for success strongly in your favor.

- *Which positive and negative fundamental forces will determine the company's future worth?* No investor should be so naive as to believe that the future for any company lacks pitfalls. But that is not the issue here. For any stock investment to produce desired returns, certain positive business developments *must* take place and certain negative business developments *must* be avoided. What are they? The positive ones are easy enough to find because Wall Street dwells on them, but the negative ones are rarely discussed.

- *Where does the company stand versus competitors in its major product or service lines?* It is amazing that many companies are researched and vigorously promoted without reference to their immediate peers. New product stories may sound promising, but what if the company is the fifth-largest in its field? Isn't it hard to believe that its stronger competitors will stand idly by without some response? What any investor should dearly love to find is evidence of a quasi-monopoly. That pursuit is greatly simplified by concentrating on those elements that truly distinguish the company from its peers.

- *What uniquely distinguishes the investment opportunity-risk ratio?* For every stock there is some combination of opportunity and risk that represents a fair appraisal of its future prospects. But, for a stock to have real appeal, that combination should be superior in some respect relative to other stocks. Finding and appreciating that difference improves your odds.

By now, you should have defined the essence of this company's investment appeal. If you can't develop a compelling picture, most probably you are reviewing an "also-ran" company. But, if satisfied, it is time to determine what must happen for this investment to succeed and where things are likely to go wrong.

The so-called ratio of opportunity to risk is hard to quantify and doesn't even exist as a hard number. When sophisticated investors talk about attractive opportunity-risk ratios they mean investments where the opportunities have superior quality and are substantially larger and more numerous than the risks. The greater the gap, the argument goes, the greater the potential for an above-average return.

How to master this illusive challenge? What it boils down to is that the opportunity and the risk are each determined by the combination of only three factors—the company's earnings, the multiple investors will pay for them, and the company's dividend disbursements. It is impossible to cover every scenario that can be drawn from these elements, but the following checklists feature those scenarios most frequently encountered.

Opportunity

Earnings

- A good trend continues.
- A poor trend reverses.
- There is an upside breakout from norm.
- The business cycle brings abnormal improvement.
- There is increased leverage from added debt.
- There is solid improvement in operating margins.
- Substantial price increases have an impact.
- There are positive changes in accounting.
- Other?

Multiplier

- The multiplier is historically low, but there's no impediment to improvement.
- There's an upward revision.

Dividend

- The rate rises above norm.
- Extras?

"Old familiar stuff"? Certainly. But hidden within these scenarios are the few critical elements required to make a particular stock investment successful. Finding them takes some serious reflection. Here's a start.

Earnings

- *A good trend continues.* Suppose that a company has been demonstrating consistent earnings growth at a superior rate. If that rate continues and if there is no change in the multiplier that investors are willing to pay for those earnings, it follows that the stock will rise accordingly.

- *A poor trend reverses.* If a company has experienced earnings difficulties, particularly if from nonrecurring causes, an earnings reversal can have a strong positive impact on market price. These are referred to as "turn-around" situations. Disbelief usually haunts these companies until the earnings improvement is actually demonstrated.

- *There is an upside breakout from norm.* Some companies, through better business efficiency, can make lasting improvements in their normal pattern of earnings. Upside breakouts like these not only attract investor interest, but they may invite upward revisions of the earnings multiplier as well.

- *The business cycle brings abnormal improvement.* The adversity of a recession often forces company managements to pare their overhead. When the business cycle reverses, these economies can produce unanticipated profits.

- *There is increased leverage from added debt.* Not every company can expand or enter new lines of business with retained earnings or raise additional capital through an equity offering. Debt has its legitimate uses. Properly employed, it can enhance earnings and surprise the skeptical and uninformed.

- *There is solid improvement in operating margins.* Sometimes efficiencies, such as the economies of larger-scale operations, the withdrawal of an overzealous competitor, penetration of lucrative foreign markets, or divisional restructuring, bring a lasting improvement in operating margins.

- *Substantial price increases have an impact.* Conditions may arise that allow prices to be increased above prevailing levels. Competitors may have hiked their prices. Or the company may have been lax in passing on to its customers the increased cost of doing business and can now do so. Or extensive introductory marketing that featured low prices may have been successfully completed so that normal pricing is now possible. And so forth.

- *There are positive changes in accounting.* Market conditions may have made the company's inventory much more valuable. The current estimates of selling and administrative costs or the need for reserves may have been too high and net earnings will benefit.

- *Other?* There are many opportunities for a positive impact on earnings. Favorable foreign currency translation is one example.

Multiplier

- *The multiplier is historically low, but there's no impediment to improvement.* Stocks fall in and out of fashion. When a stock is at the low end of its historic multiplier range, the odds are stronger that it will move toward the other pole unless some new negative has developed in the company's outlook.

- *There's an upward revision.* Sometimes there are changes in a company's activities which upgrade the quality of its earnings. Or it may have become a prospect for acquisition. Or changing activities may bring it into another industry group that normally carries a higher earnings multiplier. The possibilities are numerous.

Dividend

- *The rate rises above norm.* A more aggressive dividend rate can be interpreted, on occasion, as an indirect vote of confidence by the management in the company's future.

- *Extras?* A special dividend declaration calls attention to a company's good fortune. Although nonrecurring, it may be interpreted as the precursor of a more generous dividend policy.

At this point, you should be able to choose the combination of earnings, multiple of earnings, and dividend developments that will be *required* for this investment's success. Ignore those other niceties that merely might add to success and be careful not to overnourish your optimism.

The risks that haunt stock investments are rarely featured for fear of chilling a sale or lowering a price. However, be assured that for any equity investment there must exist combinations of earnings, multiplier of earnings, and dividend developments that will guarantee an average or below-average investment return. Some of the common hazards lurk in the following situations.

Risk

Earnings

- A more positive trend fails to materialize.
- There's an unexpected dip below forecasts.
- The business cycle brings abnormal deterioration.
- A positive trend slows or reverses.
- More shares dilute the earnings.
- Operating profit margins narrow.
- There's a large inventory loss.
- There are negative accounting changes.
- Other?

Multiplier

- An historically high multiplier is vulnerable.
- A downward revision is possible.

Dividend

- The rate falls below norm.
- Dividends are cut unexpectedly.

"Old familiar stuff"? Not really, even though they are mainly the flip side of the positive themes. Why? Because elements of risk rarely receive attention equal to those of the opportunity. In truth, they probably deserve more, since it is hard to recover from a loss. Let's look at some common elements associated with losses.

Earnings

- *A more positive trend fails to materialize.*   Portfolio managers have become so sensitive to projections of quarterly earnings that the slightest deviation from their optimistic expectations often leads to the instant liquidation of positions at substantially lower prices.

- *There's an unexpected dip below forecasts.*   Failure of company earnings to measure up to even modest anticipations will have a negative impact. Even if a company was expected to report a loss, if the loss reported is somewhat larger than forecast, the stock will be hurt.

- *The business cycle brings abnormal deterioration.*   Most businesses are in a constant state of change, either internally or from external forces. Consequently, there can be no assurance that a company's earnings may not be more severely damaged by a downturn in the business cycle than previously experienced.

- *A positive trend slows or reverses.*   While it is unrealistic to expect a company with an above-average earnings trend to continue the pace unaltered, a slowdown, when it occurs, can be a shock.

- *More shares dilute the earnings.*   Some companies seem to have a penchant for additional equity financing just as the earnings stream is about to benefit from the company's prior efforts.

Even if the reasons put forth are worthy, the effect will be negative.

- *Operating profit margins narrow.* New competitors or competitors offering either superior product or service alternatives or lower cost will force either a reduction in selling prices or increased marketing expenses. Smaller gross profit margins will be the result.

- *There's a large inventory loss.* Sometimes a company's inventory of product loses value or is so excessively large that prices must be cut substantially to distribute it. Investors will interpret either as management's fault.

- *There are negative accounting changes.* Restructuring may ultimately mean a leaner, more profitable company, but the reflection of those changes in currently reported earnings will have a negative impact.

- *Other?* A combination of developments, though small in and of themselves, can add up to a serious effect on a company's earnings power. Investors are not inclined to be tolerant, whatever the reason.

Multiplier

- *An historically high multiplier is vulnerable.* If a stock is trading near the peak of its price-earnings multiple relative to the whole market, there is an above-average risk that the multiple will move back toward the center of its range. Moreover, it can happen without a major change in the company's earnings outlook.

- *A downward revision is possible.* Suppose that a company's business is maturing. Even though the stock carried a high multiplier previously, that will not stem a readjustment to the new realities.

Dividend

- *The rate falls below norm.* If a company has been increasing its dividends at a steady rate and merely decreases the rate of increase, investors will take that as a negative sign.

- *Dividends are cut unexpectedly.* If a company has been experiencing earnings difficulties, a cut in the dividend is a reasonable expectation and may already be factored into the price of the stock. However, if the cut comes as a surprise, shareholders will prove unforgiving.

Risks can't be avoided, but they can be better comprehended. Moreover, once exposed, the risks are easier to track. Tolerance of risk is highly personal and varies widely among investors. Your pain threshold determines whether you will be able to respond to negative developments without overreacting. Being prepared for bad news helps; blind optimism is deadly.

Now that you are satisfied that the company's investment essence has strong appeal and that the opportunities exceed the risks, it is time to address other common pitfalls. Many a promising "story" has been destroyed by a mismatch between a company's irresistible potential and its financial resources. Whatever the strength of the company's promise, make sure that the wherewithal is available to ensure its attainment. Ask yourself the questions listed below.

Finances

- How sound is this company?
- Is additional financing imminent?
- Must additional equity capital be raised?

The answers to these questions could involve a lot of research and require special skills, but fortunately all that is sought is a broad overview.

- *How sound is this company?* This is a simple question without a simple answer. Financial analysis is a slow, tedious process that is best left to experienced investment analysts. However, some investment services do provide quality ratings on companies. Sometimes the quality rating on the company's debt may also provide a clue.

- *Is additional financing imminent?* There are times when a company's stock will be promoted just prior to additional financing to put it in a more positive light. A price run-up like this can be a trap.

- *Must additional equity capital be raised?* At times, it is evident that a company's undertakings are too ambitious for its finances. If further equity capital is needed, what will the timing be? Some companies plan well ahead. Others wait until the last minute with little regard for the possibility that poor market conditions might prevail at that time.

You might expect a tight relationship between higher financial quality and investment potential. It's not that straightforward. Some well-heeled companies do not deploy their financial assets to best advantage. At the other extreme, a timely financing might give a small, emerging company a much superior risk-opportunity ratio. All you want to know is, Can the company hit its business targets with its present resources?

Every good sales pitch ends with the reason to act promptly. When a stock has been hot and well touted, it's bound to look especially attractive. But it's more likely to be overpriced. Decisions to act should be unemotional and unfettered by appeals to greed. There always are, and always will be, other alternatives. Ask yourself the questions listed below before you act.

Timeliness

- Why act now?
- Who is promoting the company to the investment community?
- What is the consensus opinion of other investors?

Some investment experts argue that timing is everything. That's accurate by hindsight. Looking back, you know exactly when you should have bought and sold. However, the timing of future actions is not that simplistic.

- *Why act now?* The worst time to make a decision is when it's the easiest to do so. "Fish go after the moving lure" is a wise old market saying. To restrain your eagerness, try to imagine the other side of the transaction. Does the buyer or seller know more than you do? Are you justified in hanging on or should you correct misguided stubbornness?

- *Who is promoting the company to the investment community?* It is axiomatic that stocks don't just go up, they are "put up" by someone. Who spreads the word on the company's good fortune and explains its failings to other investors? Is it the company? (You will find a wide range of corporate policies—from defensive isolation to promotional overabundance.) Is it professional security analysts who are recognized for their expertise in the company's affairs? Is it a public relations firm that specializes in championing the company to the investment community and the financial media? Each agency can shape a different perception of the company.

- *What is the consensus opinion of other investors?* If the majority of investors hold the same opinion of a company as yours, then the profit or loss potential may already be reflected in the current price of the stock. This is particularly true for "hot" stocks.

Look at the stock's recent action. If price and volume have been moving steadily upward, the odds are that the "story" is aging. That means that heavy profit taking may lie ahead or that the stock may have landed on a long plateau of adjustment. On the other hand, a stock showing little price and volume movement out of the ordinary should pique your interest. In fact, a little twinge in your innards probably means that the stock's risks are recognized and are adjusted into its price.

A careful investor should have a feel for consensus thinking on the stock. Arguing with Street opinion isn't always wise. There is a time to go along with the crowd. One thing is certain: If you find yourself in the minority, you should be anticipating a well-above-average return. But you may be stuck with your investment for quite some time while the majority of investors slowly reverse their opinion. If the stock's trend relative to the market looks unusually strong or weak, then the crowd may have already acted.

Don't ignore the current trend of the market either. If it's easy for you to be a buyer because the market has been rising, danger lurks. If you have to force yourself to buy, chances are that the decision is on much sounder ground.

As for promoting the company to the investment community, look for the golden mean. Eschew the shrinking violets and the incessant drumbeaters. The former will leave you adrift, and the latter will attract hordes of fair-weather shareholders who will disappear at the first hint of disappointment.

Rarely do investors test the strength of their convictions. If they do, seldom will they find their convictions unwavering or uniform. But just facing the uncertainty helps focus on the final decision. Review the key ingredients, as listed below.

Confidence

- Investment essence?
- Opportunity?
- Risk?
- Finances?
- Timeliness?

This is where it all comes together. You must answer these queries with complete candor:

- *Investment essence?* Have you developed a firm grasp on the company's basic appeal as an investment?
- *Opportunity?* How certain are you that you understand what *must* go right for this investment to succeed?

- *Risk?* How sure are you that you have uncovered where the investment is *likely* to fail?

- *Finances?* Are the company's finances sound? Are they adequate enough to permit achievement of the company's business and earnings goals?

- *Timeliness?* Is now the time to act? Some opportunities are fleeting. Could the decision be delayed while you search for a better alternative?

With all the effort put into the checkoff exercise, you might expect your confidence to be heightened. Unfortunately, it's most likely that you have encountered too much uncertainty to make that possible. And anyway you should not expect to have your confidence heightened. Remember, for every buyer there's a seller with an opposing opinion derived from substantially the same basic information. In the end, you may simply be left with a strong hunch or not much more than an educated guess. Hunches and guesses do have a role in achieving the right decision—but only after the homework has been done. On the other hand, if your confidence level has sunk too low, take a pass.

You have now reached the bottom line. The hurdles have been surmounted, and it's time to act, time to go through the final checklist.

Decision

- Buy?
- Hold?
- Sell?
- Reject?
- Wait?

Avoid procrastination, but recognize there may be good reasons for either hastening or delaying your decision. Of one thing you can be assured. "Last chance" seldom applies.

Good Luck!

If the checkoff exercise has given you a lot to think about, so much the better. There is nothing simpleminded about building and maintaining an equity portfolio. The rewards make it worth the effort. If the checkoff exercise seems overwhelming, don't be dismayed. To be a successful stock investor, you must never lose sight of the essentials. The checkoff list will become easier to use as you gain experience. By concentrating on what is essential to an investment's success or failure, you can eliminate a lot of distraction. Your comfort level in volatile markets should rise because your expectations and fears will be more realistic. It's impossible to prevent all investment oversights, but, at the very least, the checkoff list will go a long way toward turning error-prone fantasies into sound judgments.

About the Authors and Illustrator

ROBERT METZ is a Harvard Nieman Fellow, award-winning financial reporter, and the best-selling author of *CBS: Reflections in a Bloodshot Eye*, as well as a dozen other books. For 17 years, he was chief financial columnist for *The New York Times*, then chief financial correspondent for FNN. He writes a nationally syndicated column for United Feature Syndicate.

GEORGE STASEN, a veteran Wall Street professional and a leading expert in venture capital and growth companies, was a founding member of the American Stock Exchange's Oversight Committee for the Emerging Company Market-place. He is chief operating officer of Supra Medical Corporation, one of the 20 companies in the initial ECM Group.

HENRY MARTIN is a cartoonist whose work appears regularly in *The New Yorker* and is syndicated nationally.

DATE DUE

R0121993234   BUSCA   332
                       .6322
                       M596

HOUSTON PUBLIC LIBRARY
CENTRAL LIBRARY

5,9/01